MIND, SET & MATCH

LIVE YOUR DNA, CREATE A WONDERFUL LIFE

Sunil Bali

MIND, SET & MATCH

Mind, Set & Match

Published 2009 by Pureformance Publishing, Duncan House, 13 Duncan Grove, Shenley Church End, Milton Keynes MK5 6HL.

Printed in Great Britain by Philtone Printing Ltd., Bristol.

Cover design and photography by Karen Parker: www.karenparker.co.uk

Editing, typesetting and layout by Tom Boyle: www.tcomms.biz

ISBN 978-0-9563332-0-9

A CIP catalogue record for this book is available from the British Library.

© Sunil Bali 2009

The right of Sunil Bali to be identified as the author of this work has been asserted by him in accordance with the Copyright, Design and Patents Act 1988.

All rights reserved. No part of this publication may be reproduced, stored in or introduced into a retrieval system, or transmitted, in any form, or by any means (electronic, mechanical, photocopying, recording or otherwise) without the prior written permission of the copyright holder. Any person who does any unauthorised act in relation to this publication may be liable to criminal prosecution and civil claims for damages.

This book is sold subject to the condition that it shall not, by way of trade or otherwise, be lent, re-sold, hired out or otherwise circulated without the publisher's prior consent in any form of binding or cover other than that in which it is published and without a similar condition including this condition being imposed on the subsequent purchaser.

Foreword

I am often asked to write testimonials or forewords for books, especially business books. Usually I decline because most of them rely on a formula of half-baked amateur psychology and re-hashed corporate garble.

I am very pleased, however, to make an exception in the case of *Mind, Set & Match*, because this is an exceptional book. It is not just the simple philosophy and practical advice that it contains – that is true of many books, though not all authors express themselves as well as Sunil.

Nor is it the unmistakeable energy which fizzes from its pages; there is an electric charge which is almost palpable and the reader cannot help but respond. It leaves you feeling good and ready for action.

Credible content and lively expression are great qualities in a book. But what I think makes *Mind, Set & Match* exceptional is that it really does have the power to change your life and create a lasting impact.

As Sunil says at the very outset, there is a huge difference between self development and shelf development. This is not just a book to be read and enjoyed, though there is no harm in doing that. At a deeper level, it is a book to be put into practice and lived out day by day.

Sunil writes from the heart. Clearly and concisely, he shows the way to realise your dreams in all their thrilling potential.

MIND, SET & MATCH

He has drawn from his personal and business experience to show how even the smallest changes in our lives can make huge differences. If you are seeking inspiration, guidance or just more clarity in your personal and business life, then this is surely a book for you.

I consider it an honour to be part of Sunil's inner circle and to see at first hand how he continues to transform the lives of individuals and organisations. He is a truly inspirational speaker, coach and leader; I am delighted, though not surprised, that he has now added 'author' to his list of achievements.

I am sure that anyone who reads this book will benefit from doing so. I know that you will enjoy reading Sunil's words and with his help can move towards living your best life.

Nigel Risner
      European Speaker of the Year
      Best selling author of *The Impact Code*

About Sunil Bali

Sunil is an expert in human behaviour, and how you can increase both your happiness and income by consistently living your DNA and expressing your authentic self. In short, the more you do who you are, the better you do.

For the last decade Sunil has been at the forefront in the field of human achievement and well-being. He has empowered individuals and organisations to maximise their potential and well-being through his inspirational speaking and coaching.

Sunil has given several hundred talks to a wide variety of companies and organisations and has transformed the lives of thousands of people from children to leaders of global organisations. Having successfully run talent management and executive coaching programmes for leading global organisations, which have delivered results, Sunil speaks with genuine authority.

He inspires individuals to reappraise their belief systems and their actions and moreover provides them with practical tools to facilitate the delivery of their desires.

Sunil's goal is to show individuals and companies how to achieve success on an ongoing basis. His unbridled energy and enthusiasm is infectious and his messages are highly thought-provoking.

Sunil 'walks his talk' and has held Board level positions with FTSE-100 and NASDAQ-listed companies. Roles include Director of Talent & Resourcing on behalf of Vodafone Group, Santander (Abbey) and Cable & Wireless Europe.

Sunil has also managed an MBO with subsequent trade sale, run a highly profitable multi-million pound recruitment business, and is a Non-Executive Director.

Sunil's first degree in Sports Science and Psychology fuelled his passion for the psychology of human achievement and well-being. As well as being a qualified Psychotherapist he possesses an MBA. He is also a Master Practitioner of Neuro Linguistic Programming (NLP), a qualified trainer of hypnosis, and a fully licensed psychometric assessor.

When he isn't speaking, Sunil lives in Buckinghamshire with his wife and two children.

To find out more information about the complete range of services available from Sunil Bali visit our website. If you would like to receive Sunil's FREE weekly e-zine, visit our website and register today.

www.sunilbali.com

Feedback from Sunil's talks consistently shows that he creates an impact which lasts and inspires individuals to take incredible action and enjoy phenomenal success:

> "The feedback that I had from your talk has been absolutely outstanding. Your blend of humour, passion and thought-provoking content was the perfect climax to our European conference."
>
> *Adrian Derx, CEO, Elan Computing*

> "I know I wrote to you straight after your speech, but three months later people are still talking about it. You created a huge shift in peoples thinking in a short space of time. I was delighted with the results."
>
> *Dr. Sam Tyson, MD, Vedicare*

> "You had us all mesmerised from start to finish. I know I speak on behalf of every single person in the room when I say that we all left motivated to change at least one thing to improve our lives."
>
> *Daniel Osmer, MD, Spectrum*

Dedication

Sudesh P. Bali

Your star shines brightly

xx

Contents

Foreword 3
About Sunil Bali 5
Acknowledgements 15

Chapter 1: Chase your Passion not your Pension

Chase Your Passion Not Your Pension 21
Self Development vs Shelf Development. 21
The Greatest Software Ever 23
Get Out of Your Own Way 24
Live to Work, or Work to Live?. 26
Psychological Handbrake 29
The Secret. 29
Reconnect to Your Passion. 31
Zero to Hero. 33

Chapter 2: Born Free

It's Natural 43
Krisis 47
"It's Not What Happens to You, It's What
You Do About It" 49
The Questions 52
Does the Shoe Fit?. 53
Unlearning 60
Whose Dream Are You Chasing?. 64
Gift to the World 64
A Winning Hand. 65

Chapter 3: Thoughts Become Reality

The Hidden Hand 69
Forgive the Past. 71
Anyway. 74
"How Do You Do That?" 75
Starve the Monkey 77

MIND, SET & MATCH

You Get What You Expect, Not What You Want 79
The World's Biggest Club 82
Unlimited Potential 84
The Power of Now 86
Detached Engagement 87
If 91
The Subconscious Mind 93
Movies of the Mind 95
Positive Affirmations 100
Clean Language 101
Blue Trees 104
Capital without Punishment 105
Personal Mastery 108

Chapter 4: Set Yourself on Fire

How to Love Mondays 115
People Buy Passion 120
Behind the Mask 122
Be Selfish 124
Man in the Mirror 125
Latin Class 126
Entertaining Angels 129
Pick More Daisies 131
Live your Values 132
Mind's Eye 134
People vs. Things 138
Start Now 139

Chapter 5: Life Rewards Action

Motion Creates Emotion 151
Amateur vs. Professional 154
Congruent Triangles 156
The Top 5% 159
Analysis Paralysis 162
Questions Are the Answer 163
Dream Support 165

CONTENTS

Networking = Not Working 167
Me Ltd. 169
Turning Lemons into Lemonade 171
86,400 Seconds 176
The Mexican Fisherman 177

Chapter 6: Resonate

Your Innate Guidance System 181
Flow 185
Now and Zen 188
The Art of the Possible 189
Control Your Energy, Control Your Life 191
Human Being vs. Human Doing 194
DIEt 197

Chapter 7: The Child Re-discovered

The Roaring Lion 203
You Don't Walk Alone 205
Today 206

Chapter 8: Final Thoughts

Quiz: Who Do You Remember? 209
Love Is 211
Live Magically 214

Contact Sunil 217

MIND, SET & MATCH

Acknowledgements

I would like to acknowledge the people who have made the greatest impact on my life and those who have allowed this dream of mine to come to fruition:

My father – the most wonderful father, brother and best friend a boy could ever hope for. You will always inspire me.

My mother, whose courage and enormous passion for life I've been fortunate enough to inherit.

Asha, my wife, who has supported and loved me from the day we first met, regardless of my faults.

My wonderful children, Yasmin and Aran, who bring me a joy and happiness beyond words. I'm so proud of you, for who you are and what you will become.

Tia and Raul, the next generation. The future is in good hands.

My extended family, aka The Harrar's:

Sunny – the brother I never had. I'm humbled by the selfless contribution you make to the lives of my family and everyone you meet.

Sarb, Simran and Rohan, for your love and friendship.

The 'outlaws', Prabha & Suresh Chandola, for your selfless and unconditional commitment to your grandchildren.

Nick Williams, for your invaluable wisdom and care.

MIND, SET & MATCH

Nigel Risner, my mentor and one of the very best speakers in the world.

Bill Mather, a very wise friend and kindred spirit.

Bill Scott, guitar teacher extraordinaire, for taking me to another place.

Carmen Kane, for helping me to see clearly what's in the mirror.

Tom Boyle, for editing and laying out the book with such care and expertise.

Luton Town Football Club, for giving me two of the happiest days of my life – the 1988 Littlewoods Cup Final, Wembley:

> Luton Town 3 Arsenal 2;
> and 14th May 1983:
> Manchester City 0 Luton Town 1.

All my teachers, colleagues and clients, both past and present: your contributions to my life, and this book, have been immense. Thank you.

...it got to come out

Well my mama didn't 'low me
Just to stay out all night long
I didn't care what she didn't 'low
I would boogie-woogie anyhow

One night I was layin' down
I heard mama 'n papa talkin'
I heard papa tell mama, let that boy
boogie-woogie
It's in him, and it got to come out
And I felt so good

John Lee Hooker

CHAPTER 1

CHASE YOUR PASSION NOT YOUR PENSION

Chase Your Passion Not Your Pension

I don't know why you've picked up this book, but I suspect it may be because you're looking to achieve more in certain areas of your life.

It might be that you're looking for more success, more money, better relationships, or more happiness.

If that's the case, then you've come to the right place.

However, a word of caution before you continue to read this book:

Self Development vs Shelf Development

Think for a moment about why you haven't got everything that you want in your life.

Whatever your answer, I can tell you one thing – what you have been doing so far has not given you the results that you want.

You need to do something different.

If, after having read this book, you're going to do the same things you've always done then there's not much point in reading it. Sure, it's a very enjoyable and inspirational book with some great stories, but nothing will change unless you decide to take some action in the direction of your dreams.

Given that there's a multi-billion dollar industry in popular

Insanity: doing the same thing over and over again and expecting different results.
Albert Einstein

psychology and self help products, you would expect to see a lot more happy and successful people out there, but the vast majority of people would rather grow their libraries at home, than grow themselves.

This book doesn't contain table-thumping rhetoric from a self-styled motivational guru, which pumps you full of adrenalin, but a few days later leaves you empty because you don't know what to do next.

It's intentionally not a weighty tome that over-intellectualises. On the contrary, it's a careful distillation that will tell you what you need to know clearly and concisely, while inspiring and motivating you to live the life that you deserve.

The numerous headings and quotes mean that it's easy to dip in and out of once you've read it. I suggest that you write your inspirations and ideas in the book as you read it.

People don't care how much you know, until they know how much you care.
John C. Maxwell

The Greatest Software Ever

We're taught many things as we grow up, not all of them conducive to our well-being, by people who project their own insecurities and inadequacies onto us.

When we buy a piece of electrical equipment it always comes with a manual on how to use it. Yet it's amazing that we're never taught how to use the greatest piece of software known to mankind – our brain, because it's our thinking that creates our reality. We really can learn how to be successful by changing our beliefs and the quality of our thinking.

The aim of the book is to show you how you really can have it all, without the need to struggle and suppress your innate passion for life.

This book will challenge your current thinking in all areas of your life and show you how to transform your thinking to achieve results that you never dreamed were possible.

It doesn't matter where you are in your life at the moment. If you're heading in the right direction that's great, but this book will help you get there a little quicker and perhaps dream a little bigger. If you're heading in the wrong direction, or perhaps you don't know what you want to do with your life, this book will help you to create the life of your dreams.

By the end of this book, you'll know how to get from where you are to where you really want to be.

**Man is not the creature of circumstances.
Circumstances are the creatures of men.**
Benjamin Disraeli

Get Out of Your Own Way

I remember the biology class at college when I studied one of the most basic living organisms on the planet – a single celled animal called an amoeba. Even the largest ones are less than 0.5mm in size and need to be examined under a microscope.

If you prod or poke an amoeba you'll see it move in the opposite direction. If you shine a light on an amoeba, it will move away from the light source. So despite being such a primitive life form, without a brain or nerves, the amoeba will change its behaviour when it doesn't get what it wants.

It's remarkable then that as human beings, at the very top of the evolutionary tree, we keep doing the same thing when we don't get the results that we want. And if this keeps happening, we then go and find someone else to blame!

The only thing that can stop you from living the life of your dreams is you. If you can learn to get out of your own way, flow with the universe and not swim against the tide, then everything that the universe has to offer is yours for the taking.

Ask yourself how badly you want to change. Do you want to carry on living the way you are or would you prefer to do things a little bit differently and have some fun along the way?

I'm not talking about huge changes. At 99 degrees Celsius, water doesn't boil. However, an extra 1% increase in temperature

Life is not to be measured by the number of breaths we take, but the moments that take our breath away.
George Carlin

creates steam – and steam can power trains weighing over 500 tonnes.

You have now within you, and have always had, everything you need to create the life that you've dreamed of. What you might not have had is the awareness, motivation, focus, or clarity to manifest your dreams.

By the end of this book you will.

**We define ourselves by the best that is in us,
not the worst that has been done to us.**
Edward Lewis

Live to Work, or Work to Live?

"Even if you win the rat race, you're still a rat."
Lily Tomlin

We are at the dawning of a new era. Our current models of the world simply aren't working. So many of us seem to live to work, rather than work to live. We continually suppress our true self, because we think we have to hold on to a steady job to pay the mortgage and the bills. Many people hold off living today and intend to start living tomorrow, when they've got a much smaller mortgage and less debt. But tomorrow never seems to happen.

The psychological contract between employer and employee is increasingly breaking down, because the values and aspirations of the individual often don't reconcile with those of the organisation. Product and business life cycles are getting shorter and shorter and the only constant is change.

So many ambitious, well intentioned people go through life rushing around at a hundred miles an hour, with never enough time in the day. In terms of their career they sometimes get what they want, but the results in other areas of their lives are often poor.

Authentic success is where you take consistent action in the direction of your dreams but you don't have to spill blood, sweat or tears. It's success that leaves you feeling happy, fulfilled and bursting with energy. There are many Type A achievers,

Anyone can conquer fear by doing those things that he fears to do.
Eleanor Roosevelt

often well-known people, who achieve career success but at a terrible cost to their health or personal relationships. There's no doubt that stressful action can deliver your desires, but in the long term it's self-defeating because it destroys you. When you pursue instant gratification what you achieve is outer success, but it's quite often at the cost of inner success, which is the quality of your experience and the quality of your life.

My wife is a GP and her surgery is frequented by a growing number of patients whose 'dis-ease' is attributable to key areas of unhappiness and discontent rather than any physical illness.

I've coached numerous senior business executives who have been earning very large sums of money working twelve hour days and most weekends under huge pressure. They seem to have it all, but it doesn't take long before they tell me how unhappy they are. Many of them are in a job that they don't want to do, their health is suffering and a real strain is being placed on their family relationships. They expend enormous amounts of energy to get themselves to somewhere that they don't actually want to be.

But there is an alternative. You do have a choice. You can stop running on the hamster wheel of life, get off and create the reality that you desire.

How do you do this? By quitting trying to be something that you're not, and becoming who you really are. When you

**We don't stop playing because we grow old,
we grow old because we stop playing.**
George Bernard Shaw

MIND, SET & MATCH

change, so does the world around you. It's as if you and the world are locked in an intimate dance, and when you lead in a different direction, it follows step. It cannot help but follow.

**The tragedy of life is not that it ends so soon,
but that we wait so long to begin it.**
W.M. Lewis

Psychological Handbrake

In recent years I've helped countless individuals to get out of their own way and, in so doing, turn their desires into reality. I get a huge sense of achievement and fulfilment when they throw their baggage of harmful conditioning and limiting beliefs out of the window, and learn to drive down the highway of life with the psychological handbrake off, headed straight for their dreams.

This is why I decided to dedicate myself to helping individuals who are genuinely seeking to make a change and live happy, fulfilled and meaningful lives.

It's my experience that people who lead wonderful lives have a hugely positive impact on those around them. They radiate energy and abundance and inspire others to do the same.

The Secret

The facts are that 96% of the money in the world is owned by 1% of the population, and one in four of us will suffer some form of mental illness at some point in our lives. Why does such a small proportion of the planet achieve success whilst the vast majority seem to wallow in mediocrity? What is the secret to success?

Well, the great secret is that there are no secrets to success.

Over 2,300 years ago, Aristotle concluded that more than anything, men and women seek happiness in all areas of their

> **Normal is not something to aspire to,**
> **it's something to get away from.**
> Jodie Foster

lives. The things that we value most like health, relationships and money are only valued because we think that they will make us happy. While the world has changed a lot since the time of Aristotle, our deep-rooted desire for success and happiness remains undiminished.

Research by an army of psychologists from all over the world clearly shows that life's true achievers, from Buddha to Bill Gates and Lance Armstrong to Leonardo da Vinci, have all had one thing in common – the quality of their thinking. True achievers have beliefs which empower them. These beliefs lead them to think the right thoughts, which result in the right actions which, in turn, produce the right results.

If you want to achieve more, then you need to challenge your current beliefs and thinking. Unfortunately, millions of people don't fulfil their desires because they believe that there's nothing they can do to change their lot. This simply isn't true. As Napoleon Hill said in his book *Think and Grow Rich*, "Whatever the mind of man can conceive and believe, it can achieve."

As long as I have to die my own death, I have decided to live my own life and not let others live it for me.
Hanoch McCarthy

Reconnect to Your Passion

"If you can't do it with feeling, don't."
Patsy Cline

Success doesn't happen by accident. It's a process which starts by listening to your heart, then using your head. It doesn't work the other way around, because the head is conditioned to "do the right thing" and conform to the conventions of society. This makes your ego feel good.

The heart on the other hand, will always reconnect you to your passion. If you follow your heart and take action, then you have to be successful. It's a universal law, just like the law of gravity.

When you throw a ball up in the air, it has to come down. It doesn't matter who threw the ball, how intelligent they are, how old they are, whether they are a good or a bad person, the ball will always come back down.

It's only by expressing your true nature, your authentic self, that you can be both happy and successful.

By successful, I mean being free to do what you want and leading a happy and fulfilled life. Notice that there is no mention of money in my definition of success. This is because happiness is the key to success. Success is not the key to happiness. When you're happy and doing what you love, the money will flow to you.

It's never too late to be the person you could have been.
George Eliot

In short, the more you do who you are, the better you'll do.

When you're passionate about what you do, your overwhelming energy will break through any barriers and obstacles that appear in your way, and you'll attract everything you need to be successful.

When you're happy and bursting with energy, you'll leverage the world around you by resonating with everyone and everything in it. By spending time "in the zone", as sportsmen call it, you'll be in flow with everyone and everything around you and so deliver results in all areas of your life without struggle.

It's when you're able to control your energy that you can control where your life is heading.

We are all born originals – why is it so many of us die copies?
Edward Young

Zero to Hero

I do a lot of public speaking on the subject of success, because it's a subject that's very close to my heart and one that I'm passionate about.

I'm the son of first generation Indian migrants who came over to England in the early Sixties. In a foreign land with very few friends, the most important thing for them was to have security for the family: a roof over their heads with a steady job to put food on the table.

As many of my Indian contemporaries will acknowledge, the children of these migrants were under enormous pressure to increase the status of their family in the community by becoming the ultimate professional … a doctor.

The problem was that, come my A-levels, the fairer sex and sport captured far more of my attention than the periodic table ever could. Even though English was by far my best subject at school, I was instructed by 'she who must be obeyed' (my mother) to take three sciences at A-level as this was the best way to become a doctor.

It came as no great surprise, therefore, that I never managed to comprehend the intricacies of quantum physics and my grades were just about good enough to secure a university place studying Sports Science and Psychology.

My mother was very disappointed, but relieved as I had at least got into university and not a polytechnic. Otherwise she

> **We make a living by what we get, but we make a life by what we give.**
> Winston Churchill

MIND, SET & MATCH

would have had to hide away for three years until I left such a second rate establishment. If truth be told, it was one of the very few courses that would accept me and I was not too displeased as the syllabus actually seemed quite interesting. But what does one do when one leaves university armed with such a degree?

Well, my mother wanted me to become an accountant. So off I went to work at our local County Council with a place on their graduate finance scheme, leading to qualification as an accountant.

Eighteen months into the scheme, having barely scraped through two sets of exams, it became clear that for me accountancy was as about as interesting as watching paint dry. I would have left much earlier, but I had already let my mother down by not becoming a doctor. Now I couldn't even accomplish the next best thing and become an accountant.

However, my employer was very reasonable and quite understanding, given that I'd wasted 18 months of their time and money, and let me transfer onto the graduate IT scheme. But 18 months later, guess what – structured systems analysis and design methodologies had a hypnotic effect on me. My employer and I parted company by mutual consent.

So in the space of three years I had managed to drop out of two graduate trainee schemes. I was now unemployed at a time when the graduate job market was at its worst for many

**Life is either a daring adventure
or nothing.**
Helen Keller

years. My confidence and self-esteem were at an all-time low and my situation seemed hopeless. I felt that I was on the scrapheap at the tender age of 25.

I managed to get a job selling advertising space for a magazine, but after four weeks I hadn't sold a single ad. I left before they asked me to. To compound matters, I was being compared by my mother and relatives to three of my cousins of similar age who had become a dentist, accountant and solicitor.

After a few weeks of being unemployed I secured a job in recruitment. There was no great career plan at this stage. I was just thankful to be in a job.

It wasn't a particularly stimulating job, but at least this was something I could do. I was completely driven by the need to be recognised as a success by my mother and relatives and I worked incredibly hard.

I had only been in the job for two months when my father died suddenly at the age of 54. I had an exceptionally good relationship with my father, who had always told me to do whatever I wanted to do, but be the very best that I could be in my chosen vocation. However, his wise words were drowned out by mother who maintained a vice-like grip on all the decisions that were made in our house.

At this point I thought to myself, what's the point in worrying? What more can go wrong? I'm just going to enjoy what I do and if I don't, then I'm not going to do it. The result was that

A wise man knows that he has only one enemy – himself.
Ben Hecht

within the space of just over three years I went from being unemployed to becoming the Director of Talent & Resourcing for Cable & Wireless, a $10 billion turnover company, managing a spend of over $100m. I had also completed an MBA which the company paid for.

This was immediately followed by a multi-million dollar management buy-out and my earnings had gone from zero to over $500k per year. At last I was getting the approval that I craved from my mother.

My last two roles were as Director of Talent & Resourcing of two of Europe's largest and most successful companies, Vodafone Group and Abbey, part of the Santander group.

I don't tell this to impress you, but rather to impress upon you that once you actively follow your passion, the success looks after itself.

But then suddenly one day I gave it all up and phoned all the head-hunters telling them that I was leaving mainstream work and wouldn't be coming back. At the time I was managing a team of nearly 100 people, earning a six figure salary and responsible for hiring over 5,000 people a year.

So what made me do this? Had I gone mad?

Well, let me tell you about the week prior to my resignation.

At the beginning of the week, on Sunday evening, my wife checked my blood pressure as I had been feeling very tired

We teach people how to treat us.
Philip McGraw

for several weeks. I put it down to working very long hours and pressure at work. Being a couple of stones overweight didn't help, but I didn't have time to exercise and meal-time usually meant a sandwich on the run or a take-away on the late train just before I went to bed.

I was shocked to learn that my blood pressure was sky high and my resting heart rate was considerably higher than it should be. "You're suffering from stress," my wife announced. "But I don't do stress," I retorted in my best Neanderthal voice.

That week, as part of the overall talent management programme, I had arranged to see several of the directors, in complete confidence, to canvass their opinions on how the introduction of an executive coaching programme might help them.

By the middle of the week there was a distinct pattern emerging in their feedback. Despite being very well paid, over 80% of them were complaining of working very long hours, feeling exhausted and stressed, all of which was having a negative impact on their family life.

I went home that night and told my wife. "Why are you surprised?" she said. "They're just the same as you. Nearly half of my patients come to me with symptoms that are related to workplace stress."

The following day I noticed that one of the Finance Directors had cancelled our meeting. I phoned his PA, rather annoyed

It wasn't raining when Noah built the Ark.
Howard Ruff

at this late cancellation, to be told: "Graham has had a massive heart attack and is in intensive care, critically ill."

That day's meetings revealed more severely stressed directors. At the end of the day I met with the HR team to compare notes as they were conducting a similar exercise with a view to providing coaching at middle management level. The results were no different – over two thirds of the managers were stressed out, would rather be doing something they were really passionate about and felt that the only reason for coming to work was to pay the bills.

So much doom and gloom. Anyway, the following day was Friday and in the evening I went to Wembley to watch England vs. Brazil with three of my mates. What should have been a wonderful evening turned very sour 20 minutes into the first half.

I suddenly felt a sharp pain in my knee and at first thought that someone was attacking me. What had actually happened was that a man had fallen into my aisle seat and then hit his head on the concrete floor. It became clear very quickly that this man had either suffered a heart attack or a brain haemorrhage as his pupils were fixed and dilated and his breathing, at first shallow, had actually stopped.

The medics managed to get a very weak pulse with the use of a defibrillator before he was stretchered away, barely breathing and unconscious. As this happened I overheard one of the

If opportunity doesn't knock, build a door.
Milton Berle

group he had been with utter, "He's got such a stressful job — his wife's been telling him for ages to take things easy."

To make the whole experience even more traumatic, the man bore an uncanny resemblance to my father and his teenage son was not dissimilar in appearance to me when I was younger.

I suddenly realised that this scene could easily have been me and my son, and that the events of the week were clearly trying to tell me something.

There were 88,000 people in the stadium that day, so there was a 1 in 88,000 chance that the man would collapse into my lap. And then what were the chances that the father and son would bear such a striking resemblance to me and my father?

The incident reduced me to tears and as I wandered behind the stand trying to compose myself, I suddenly realised that I had got my priorities all wrong. My whole identity and self-worth were wrapped up in trying to maintain a job that was actually killing me.

There was no time for fun in my life. My wife and kids were lucky to see me at all during the week, and only a pale, exhausted imitation of the real me at the weekend.

I thought back to that last time that I had been both happy and successful a few years earlier when I had managed a multi-million pound management buy-out. The difference was clear: I had stopped doing what I loved. While my pride

Never mistake motion for action.
Ernest Hemingway

and sense of service drove me to do a good job and add value wherever possible, every day was like swimming uphill in treacle with one hand tied behind my back. I had absolutely no passion for my work.

Within six months of leaving my job I had lost over 25 lbs in weight and my blood pressure returned to normal. I spent quality time with my family, started learning to play blues guitar – something I had always wanted to do – played football every week and saw much more of my friends, who told me that I was looking much younger and happier.

I'm now completely passionate about my work, and continue to do those things that make me happy, like playing blues guitar, sport and spending quality time with friends and family. I've rediscovered how great it feels to be fit and healthy and have not only managed to keep the weight off, but have a six pack – not bad for a 46 year old!

Dreams don't die until we let them.
James Ojala

CHAPTER 2

BORN FREE

It's Natural

We start out as champions. Our innate ability leads us to master complicated things like language and locomotion. Imagine if we were to give up learning to walk the first few times we fell down? The human species would never have evolved beyond a species of bottom shufflers!

We're born with the mindset to achieve whatever our heart desires.

Every year I speak in schools to groups of 10-year-olds who are about to go to secondary school, and to groups of 16-year-olds who are about to choose subjects for their A-level exams. I love doing this as it's hugely rewarding to work with young people and to be able to inspire and motivate them. Before I explain why and how they can be, do or have anything they want, I like to gauge the mindset of my audience. One of the ways I do this is by putting up the following words:

opportunityisnowhere

It's revealing that in the 10-year-old group, typically over 80% of the students say they see:

opportunity is now here

However, in what is a sad indictment of our society today, in the group of 16-year-old students, typically over 60% say that they see:

opportunity is nowhere

Every child is born a genius.
Albert Einstein

A 300% increase in negative mindsets in only six years!

I should also point out that there are always a few children in both groups who see:

opportunity i snow here !

Research tells us that children up to pre-school age laugh about 300 times a day. 300 times! It's because to them life is one big happy event. They have what they need and aren't concerned in the least about what they don't have. Children are experts in the art of happiness. They're happy to see mum and dad, so they smile and laugh. They're happy to see their lunch, so they smile and laugh. They're happy to play with a ball, so they smile and laugh. They're happy!

As adults, we laugh about 15 times a day.

So where does it go wrong?

It has been estimated that by the time we are 18 years old we will have been praised, supported and encouraged about 2,500 times – and 50% of these occasions will have been before the age of three! By the time we reach 18 we will also have been criticised, scolded, belittled, or told we're stupid around 22,500 times – a ratio of 9:1. No wonder we grow up with a negative mindset and low self-esteem that hampers us for the rest of our lives.

From the very earliest days of man, philosophers, mystics and prophets have unequivocally said that a blissful state of

Life expands or diminishes in proportion to one's courage.
Anais Nin

being is our natural birthright. We don't actually need to do anything to rediscover our true joyous nature – except to become aware of how we're blocking it.

When we were babies and very young children we knew what we wanted. We may have smiled, chuckled or waved our arms and legs to show this, or cried, bawled and stamped our feet. As we grow older we forget what we want and start to fulfil the expectations of others. It could be parents who want us to become a professional, maybe a doctor, accountant or lawyer as these tend to be secure, well paid and well regarded individuals.

We respond to our conditioning and adopt a persona to please others. We try to win the approval of those above us. At work we try not to upset the boss and feel driven to conform to company ideals. We are, however, not our conditioning. If we are to be whole and happy we need to reconnect.

We waste so much time and energy trying to be someone else just to please others. These behaviours are at odds with our true self and how we really want to be. As a result we start to feel frustration, anger and resentment. The longer we repress our true nature, the more discontented we become and the more susceptible we are to ill health.

The ancient people of Hawaii had a philosophy of living called Huna. Within this system of teaching is the concept that we keep 'black bags' in our bodies. In the black bag are

> **It is wisdom to know others, it is enlightenment to know oneself.**
> Tao Te Ching

MIND, SET & MATCH

the unresolved emotions from previous unhappy experiences. Occasionally, our subconscious mind will bring the black bag to the surface and try and to open it, so that we can resolve this unhappiness at the conscious level.

If we don't address the issues that cause our unhappiness, if we repress the innate urge to seek happiness, then Huna teaches that disease will manifest itself.

Research into the effects of stress shows that prolonged stress has a severely debilitating effect on the body and is the root cause of much of the prevailing illnesses in the 21st century.

Genuine success is the kind of success where you get what you want, without damage to your health or emotional well-being. When you get really clear and honest about what you want, it's quite amazing how everything in the world conspires to help you get it.

Remember that you are unique, and if that is not fulfilled, then something has been lost.
Martha Graham

Krisis

More people die before 9am on a Monday morning than at any other time of the week. Researchers at Columbia University have shown that the number one risk factor for a fatal heart attack is not being overweight, smoking, having high cholesterol or high blood pressure, but being unhappy in your job.

As humans we need to work. We need a channel to expend our energy, to express our creative nature, to give value and meaning to our lives. If this channel is blocked, there is a build-up of stress which manifests over time in poor mental and physical health. We may reach a crisis point, but often we return to bad habits once the crisis has passed.

The word *crisis* comes from the Greek verb *krinein* which means to separate, judge or make a decision. We reach crisis because we haven't listened to our innate guidance system. Instead we have played it safe by joining the rat race and setting our own rat trap.

We feel that it's easier to conform, to do what is expected of us. That way we avoid disapproval, whether from parents, bosses, friends, relatives or the public at large. The truth is that it's massively more dangerous to abandon our desires than follow our dreams and immerse ourselves in work that we love.

Whatever traumas and injustices life may have heaped upon

> It is the characteristic of the ego that it takes all that is unimportant
> as important, and all that is important as unimportant.
>
> Meher Baba

us, the past should be nothing more than a reference point. It is not a place where we should reside. History is full of examples of people who have overcome great hardship and adversity to create the life that they want.

A musician must make his music, an artist must paint, a poet must write if he is to ultimately be at peace with himself.
Abraham Maslow

"It's Not What Happens to You, It's What You Do About It"

Take the story of one of my fellow professional speakers, the great American, W. Mitchell.

Mitchell was 28, just an ordinary guy who loved his newly acquired 750cc motorcycle, when something terrible happened to him. One day while out riding he was struck by a laundry truck whose driver had failed to see him at a junction. The impact not only broke several bones, it also dislodged the motorbike's fuel cap. Mitchell was drenched in petrol. The fuel ignited, transforming him into a human bonfire.

Mitchell's life was saved by a witness who managed to put out the flames with an extinguisher. He woke up in the burns unit of San Francisco General Hospital with second, third and fourth degree burns to 65% of his body. Fourth degree burns are so severe that muscles, ligaments and bones have been damaged. His face was unrecognisable, his hands irreparably damaged. Doctors doubted that he would survive.

We can only imagine the excruciating, incessant pain he experienced. Doctors agree that the pain associated with this kind of burn is the most intense that humans can experience. Yet Mitchell was unusually motivated. The first thing he said on learning that his hands were useless was, "This is gonna really screw up my pool game." His courage and determination were evident from the moment he regained consciousness.

**It's better to do your own work imperfectly,
than do the work of another perfectly.**
Bhagavad Gita

Four months later he left the hospital. Disfigured, his return to city life was far from pleasant. Unsettled by the constant stares and thoughtless comments, he decided to move. He relocated to a town in Colorado where his upbeat spirits quickly led him to make many new friends. It didn't take much longer for Mitchell to co-found a multi-million dollar business, buy a beautiful house, obtain a pilot's licence and even own an airplane.

Despite huge challenges, his courage and can-do attitude led to a successful, fulfilling life. That isn't the end of the story, though.

One winter's day he set off for a flight in his airplane with some friends. Ice on the wings caused the plane to crash shortly after take-off. Miraculously no-one was killed and everyone managed to get out quickly – except for Mitchell. At first he thought his feet were stuck. Then he couldn't feel his legs. His back suddenly started to hurt sharply. An ambulance rushed him to hospital, where he would later learn that his spine was broken and he would never walk again.

W. Mitchell had experienced his second life-altering accident. Not only disfigured and missing most of his hands, he was now paralysed from the waist down and confined to a wheelchair for life.

Try to imagine his emotional state. Such unbelievable adversity – how much can one person take? Yet once again

Men are not disturbed by things that happen, but by their opinions of things that happen.
Epictetus

Mitchell fought back, his spirit unquenched. His attitude is summed up by a comment he made during his time in the hospital: "Before I was paralysed there were 10,000 things I could do; now there are 9,000. I can either dwell on the 1,000 I've lost or focus on the 9,000 I have left."

While in hospital he learned that a mining company wanted to dig a huge, ugly hole in the beautiful mountain that overlooks his town. The news seemed to spur his recovery. To stop the mining work he decided to run for mayor, and eventually served for two consecutive terms. He was also successful in convincing the company that drilling the mountain wasn't such a great idea after all.

Mitchell is fond of saying "it's not what happens to you, it's what you do about it." He is a living example of what will-power, courage and determination can achieve against all odds. His body may be in a wheelchair, but his spirit is free. I find his story inspirational. It reminds me that circumstances alone do not determine the quality of your life. What truly matters is your attitude.

At the time of writing, W. Mitchell owns several successful businesses and is an exceptional motivational speaker who has won worldwide acclaim. He even enjoys adventure activities such as water rafting and skydiving.

After all there are still 9,000 things left to do.

Nothing can bring you peace but yourself.
Ralph Waldo Emerson

The Questions

At some point in their life, everyone is confronted by the following two questions:

"Who am I?"

"Why am I here?"

Most of us never pause for long enough to answer these important questions. In so doing we resign ourselves to a life of routine, punctuated by brief periods where we numb the pain - the annual holiday, binge drinking or just countless hours in front of the television.

So many of us just seem to live for the weekend, even though this represents such a small part of our time on Earth.

By taking jobs which don't make us happy but simply pay the bills, we turn ourselves into slaves.

Nothing has a stronger influence on children than the unlived lives of their parents.
Carl Jung

Does the Shoe Fit?

The important thing to realise is that you have a choice. Your life doesn't have to unfold in this way. A more creative and imaginative path is waiting for you. All you need to do is take a deep breath and step forward.

The more you rely on yourself, the more confidence you will have. The more you take responsibility for where you are and you are going, the better you will become in achieving the results you want.

Over the years I've been responsible for hiring thousands of people for a variety of companies, from board level executives to receptionists. The one thing that never ceases to amaze me is that people work so hard and try so hard to get a job which really doesn't suit them, and which isn't something that they really want to do.

It reminds me of going to a shoe sale. You find a pair of shoes at an absolute bargain price, but they're half a size too small. No matter what you do, these shoes aren't ever going to fit properly. If you wear shoes that don't fit you, they are going to cause you discomfort and pain. They might stretch a bit, but ultimately they're never really going to be right for you.

It's similar with your work. It has to be right for you, because when it's right for you it will fit you like a glove – and you'll love it.

To be independent of public opinion is the first formal condition of achieving anything great.

Georg Hegel

I used to be responsible for the graduate recruitment programme for Cable & Wireless, a very large global blue-chip company, and usually attended the last stage of the process, a candidate's final interview.

One of the entry streams was for the Finance Management scheme, where the company sponsored graduates to train as accountants while gaining valuable work experience. Within five or six years of joining the scheme, the entrants would have qualified and be well on their way to running their own business unit. Essentially, we were hiring the leaders of tomorrow.

The scheme also involved an overseas posting to destinations such as the Caribbean, Seychelles and Maldives, where Cable & Wireless was the primary provider of telecommunications. Add to this a very generous salary, bonus, car, study leave and holiday entitlement and you won't be surprised to know that we typically had over fifty applicants for each place on the scheme.

Most applicants did not get through the initial screening, where the selection criteria included outstanding academic qualifications and evidence of a well-rounded individual, typically identified by non-academic extracurricular activity such as sports, music, drama or membership of clubs and societies. If they were selected for assessment they then faced a full day of interviews, psychometric testing, role plays and presentations.

**Our doubts are traitors and make us lose the good
we oft might win by fearing to attempt.**
William Shakespeare

The evening before the final interviews, I took home a folder with the CVs and assessment results of the candidates I would be meeting the next day.

While all the finalists had very strong profiles and assessment scores, one candidate, a physics undergraduate, seemed quite exceptional. Not only had he always scored straight 'A' grades, but he had won prizes throughout his academic career for outstanding achievement, including his first two years at university. His Professor at Oxford had written a glowing recommendation, stating that he was probably the best student that he had ever come across in nearly twenty years of teaching. As if this wasn't enough, he also played tennis at county level, was a member of the National Youth Theatre and edited a student newsletter.

I was looking forward to meeting this rising star. It seemed a formality that we would offer him a place. I thought my primary concern at the interview would be selling the opportunity to him, as there were sure to be other companies keen to secure his services.

As it turned out, his was the last interview of the day. We've saved the best till last, I thought.

After the usual formalities, about a quarter of an hour into the interview, I noticed that his mood was a little flat and didn't seem completely enthused by the prospect of joining us. I asked if he had offers from other companies and he told

Look within. Within is the fountain of good and it will ever bubble up, if you will ever dig.
Marcus Aurelius

me in a lazy drawl that he had seen three other companies and they had all offered him contracts to train as an accountant.

When I asked why he was interested in accountancy, he gave the stereotypically correct answers. But I was concerned that while he said all the right things, the body language betrayed a lack of enthusiasm.

"I notice that your father's an accountant," I said. "What does he feel about you following in his footsteps?"

"He's always been keen for me to become an accountant because it's a well respected, secure, well paid job", he replied.

This didn't seem like the same chap who a week earlier at the assessment day had given an electrifying presentation about the universe entitled "The First 15 Billion Years in 15 Minutes."

"Would you mind if I digress for a few moments?" I said to him. "I'm very interested in the universe and missed your presentation."

It was as if his chair had been plugged into the mains. His posture went from slumped to bolt upright, like a meerkat on heat. His eyes were now wide open, his movements became very animated and his voice went up an octave.

What ensued was a quite fascinating half hour, where he proceeded to identify and then fill in the considerable gaps in my knowledge. He was like a master storyteller holding court. I was spellbound.

The way to be happy is to make others so.
Robert Ingersoll

At the end of our conversation I leaned forward and said, "OK, cards on the table. If you want a job here, the job's yours. You probably know that anyway. But let me ask you just one final thing: if your father was happy for you to follow any career, what would you do?"

"I've always been fascinated by outer space since my dad bought me a book on astronomy when I was seven," he said. "My dream job would be to work at the forefront of space exploration and research, so it would have to be as a scientist for NASA.

"My father had a very hard childhood and came from a very poor family. He dragged himself out of the gutter by working all hours and then going to night school to become an accountant. He has worked so hard to look after me and my family and put me through private school. My father cried with happiness when I won a place at Oxford. I just want to make him happy. He deserves it."

As he finished his sentence he looked towards the floor, his voice breaking with emotion.

When he looked up I replied, "I suspect what your father wants more than anything else is for you to be happy. It's just that he's not aware that there's another route to happiness for you which doesn't require you to become an accountant.

"How about we do a deal? I'll send you a letter offering you a place on our Finance Scheme and you talk to your father

You can have everything in life if you can just help others to get what they want.
Zig Ziglar

about how you felt when you read the book he bought you when you were seven, and why you love astronomy."

"It's a deal", he said with a smile on his face.

Later that month I looked at the list of people who had accepted a place on the scheme and saw that the name of our number one candidate was absent. I thought that he had probably succumbed to the advances of a high-paying merchant bank and promptly forgot about him.

Well, nearly three years later I was just about to leave my office for a meeting when my PA arrived with my post. Anything deemed important I asked her to thrust under my nose. "You should read this before you go," she said.

I noticed that it was half a page of very neat copperplate handwriting which would only take a few seconds to read.

The next few seconds were among the most rewarding that I ever experienced in my corporate career:

There's always one moment in life when the door opens and lets the future in.
Graham Greene

Dear Mr. Bali

It's been many moons since we met and you may not remember our conversation about the very same, when you interviewed me for a place on your Graduate Finance Scheme over two years ago.

As a result of our conversation that day and the agreement that I made with you, I had a wonderful heart to heart with my father.

I thought you would be interested to know that I will receive my PhD this summer and have been awarded a post-doctoral fellowship in astrophysics by NASA. My father is very proud of me and so am I!

I'm looking forward to heading off to Washington DC, to see more of the world…quite literally.

Thank you so very much for your 'advice'. It changed my life.

Kindest regards

Be faithful to that which exists nowhere but in yourself.
André Gide

MIND, SET & MATCH

Unlearning

The 1833 Abolition of Slavery Act was supposed to end slavery. But I guarantee that if you walk into any large company building in the UK, you'll see that slavery not only still exists but is very much alive and flourishing.

Having been responsible for managing talent in some very large companies, there is a picture that I'm unfortunately all too familiar with. It's the sight of countless people sitting in their cubicles wishing the clock would go faster and work its way round to the magic hour when it's time to go home.

A friend of mine who owns a multi-million dollar property company once said to me that JOB stands for "Just Over Broke." Given that after 40 years in employment, it's been estimated that less than 1% of people have enough money to enjoy an adequate retirement, what is the point of flogging yourself to death in a job that you don't want to do, and which doesn't pay you enough?!

So is it the fault of the employers? No, not at all.

In fact, there are more and more employers who are trying to create a business culture where individuals can be creative, express themselves and meet personal objectives while fulfilling those of the organisation.

We are our own jailers and have completely forgotten that we locked the door. But we still have the keys to freedom. We

That which does not kill us makes us stronger.
Nietzsche

can't blame anyone else. We have to take responsibility for our own situation, whether this be a heaven or a hell.

Interestingly, the word 'hell' is derived from an Old English word that means a fence or a pen to keep animals in. Our hell is created by the limiting beliefs with which we resolutely ensnare ourselves.

When I was in India a few years ago I was taken to an elephant sanctuary. Here, orphaned or ill elephants were nurtured back to health and in return for their keep they helped with the logging. I couldn't help noticing a large circular piece of grassland where some of the elephants seemed to be corralled, but with no barrier to contain them and no keeper to stop them straying. The circle was marked out with white paint, but there was nothing actually stopping the elephants from crossing the white line and making a break for freedom. Rather bizarrely, this white circle had a wooden gate at one end fixed to two wooden stakes, but there was not a fence in sight!

I noticed that one of the younger elephants had one foot cuffed to a long chain, which was attached to a large wooden post at the centre of the circle.

I asked one of the elephant keepers why the elephants never crossed the white line, and only ever left the circle with a keeper through the pointless wooden gate.

"It's really quite simple," he replied. "When an elephant first

Put your future in good hands – your own.
Mark Victor Hansen

MIND, SET & MATCH

arrives it's chained to the centre post and can go no further than the edge of the circle, as this is as far as the chain will go. After a few weeks we remove the chain but the elephant is conditioned to think that the white line is as far as it can ever go, so it never attempts to cross it.

This story is true of so many of us. It is our beliefs that limit where we go and what we think we can achieve.

Harry Houdini used to have a small cage from which he used to escape with seemingly effortless ease, time and time again.

There was only one occasion when Houdini couldn't escape from the cage. He tried for hours and hours but eventually, completely exhausted, he gave up. And the reason that he couldn't escape? The door was open all the time and had never been locked. So the only time that Houdini failed to escape was when the cage was actually open. His mindset was so attuned to being trapped that he was trapped even when he was free!

What a great metaphor this is for our lives. We can walk out of our self-made prisons at any time. All we need is the awareness to change our mindsets.

Michelangelo was once asked: "How do you create such beautiful statues and models?"

His replied: "I simply start with a block of stone and chip away all that isn't the beauty that I want."

Everyone thinks of changing the world, but no one thinks of changing himself.
Leo Tolstoy

This is how it is with our conditioning. Our job is to chip away at the beliefs which lead us to think negative, unproductive thoughts which obscure our true nature.

We don't have to re-create ourselves, but simply unlearn that which isn't true. We're born as champions, but become conditioned by those around us to fail in our quest for happy and fulfilled lives.

By taking on board the values, beliefs, attitudes and opinions of others, we repress our true spirit. If we are to live the life of our dreams, then we have to undo our conditioning and discard the values and beliefs that hinder our quest.

This negative conditioning restricts the amount of energy that we have available to us to focus on those actions that will manifest that which we desire.

It is futile to blame others for the excess baggage that we carry, whether they are parents or teachers. In most cases they were doing the best they could with the resources available to them.

Or, as one of the fundamental tenets of NLP (Neuro-Linguistic Programming) says, "there is no such thing as unresourceful people, only unresourceful states."

**When heart and skill work together,
expect a masterpiece.**
C. Reade

Whose Dream Are You Chasing?

Most people spend their lives chasing someone else's dreams, then wind up disappointed that they never achieve them – or even more disappointed when they do.

It's a strange phenomenon of life that the majority of people give up on their dreams. They devote their time, energy and talents towards fulfilling someone else's dream, while their own slowly dies inside them.

If you leave your dreams in someone else's hands, guess what they have planned for you? Not as much as you have.

Think about your work. Whose dreams are you chasing?

Gift to the World

Settling for too little, rather than wanting too much, is at the root of many people's problems. When we lead a life where we don't fulfil our potential, we send a clear message to our children that it's OK to settle for second best.

If you've got kids, it's so important to break the chain. One of the greatest gifts that you can give to the world is children who are bursting with energy and passion to fulfil their dreams.

So keep it real for your kids and leave the world a priceless legacy: children who are alive.

You don't get harmony when everyone sings the same note.
Doug Floyd

A Winning Hand

Both in my corporate career and also in my coaching practice, I often ask people if they think that life is fair. I rarely get a straight "yes" or "no" answer, but it quickly becomes clear that many of them feel that life has dealt them a losing hand, so life is unfair to them.

I then surprise them by agreeing that life isn't fair, and demonstrating that the cards are stacked heavily in their favour. Life has dealt you a winning hand. The reason that most people are unsuccessful is that they simply don't play their hand. They keep it to themselves and still expect to win.

If you express who you really are and do the work that you were born to do, there can only be one result: you will be successful and happy.

Even if you're on the right track, you'll get run over if you just sit there.
Will Rogers

MIND, SET & MATCH

CHAPTER 3

THOUGHTS BECOME REALITY

The Hidden Hand

Let me ask you to consider the following question:

Does grass try to grow?

I'm not trying to be deliberately obtuse, but merely want you to consider how, without the intervention of man, this happens.

I was doing some training at a seminar once, but kept getting interrupted by a chap in the audience when I talked about the need to have faith or trust. "Look," he said, "I'm really inspired by what you've said but I have a real problem with all this talk about faith and trust in something greater than ourselves."

Now I wasn't specifically talking about God, but rather the fact that there seems to be a hidden hand behind some of the magic that occurs in the universe. And if you do take the right action and allow this benevolent universe or God or whatever you want to call it to help you, then it finds ways to do exactly that. The number of positive synchronistic events seems to increase markedly and you attract the people, resources and answers to help you to achieve your aims.

It was nearly the coffee break but I could hear this chap muttering under his breath. Clearly he was not happy.

There was a bunch of flowers on the table which included a beautiful red rose. I went over to the vase, picked out the

Your thoughts are a preview of life's coming attractions.
Albert Einstein

rose and presented it to my critic. As I gave it to him I said, "Could you please make me one of those?"

He looked at me a little puzzled for a few seconds. Then a smile slowly appeared on his face and he said: "I know what you mean now."

So as well as having faith in yourself, try to have faith and trust in the universe and see what happens.

A very pleasant surprise awaits you.

**If you can dream it,
you can do it.**
Walt Disney

Forgive the Past

As a personal and professional coach and also as a psychotherapist, I've heard many horrifying accounts of people's pasts. These include child abuse cases, wife battering, a partner and children being killed. You get the picture.

No matter what our past holds, we can't continue to live there. The past should not be a place of residence. It's a reference point from which we must learn and grow.

Rarely do we achieve what we want by hanging on to what happened to us in the past. We need to ask ourselves, "What do I need to know, that if I knew it, I could forgive the past?"

Take the instance of my mother. My mother has always had huge energy and drive, which she instilled in me, but she also had incredibly high expectations of what I should achieve academically. So there was a lot to live up to when I was growing up. If I ever fell short of these expectations – which was often, as I had no interest in becoming a doctor – our relationship became difficult as my mother would always refer to those of my peers who had done better than me. Hence as a child I felt that I wasn't good enough.

This cloud of 'not being good enough' hung over me well into my twenties and early thirties, resulting in considerable mental turmoil. One day I sat down and spoke to my grandmother who had recently migrated to this country. It suddenly dawned on me that my mother was simply exhibiting

> **Let me not pray to be sheltered from dangers but to be fearless in facing them.**
>
> Tagore

the same behaviour that her parents had shown her when she was growing up.

Everyone is doing the best they can with the resources they have available. The behaviour that people exhibit is the one they feel will best serve them at that particular time.

As a first generation migrant, my mother valued security very highly. She thought that the best way for me to be secure was to have a safe, well paid and well respected job, and at the top of her wish list was 'doctor'.

Once I knew that my mother genuinely wanted the best for me, and I realised that she was conditioned to believe there was only one way to achieve this, then our relationship improved dramatically.

Many parents have a lot to answer for, but only because their parents were messed up as well!

Explore your past and identify who and what you need to forgive. By holding on to anger, sadness or guilt, you're hurting yourself and those you love.

All negative thoughts and all negative emotions such as anger, sadness and guilt are based on fear. When we're angry it's because we feel that we need to control a person or situation. This is quite futile.

I come across many relationships where one partner tries to control what the other partner does or says. Once the

No man enjoys the true taste of life but he who is ready and willing to quit it.
Seneca

domineering partner focuses on supporting the other person's needs and trying to fulfil those needs, rather than trying to control them through anger, the need for control melts away. Gratitude and respect start to enter the relationship, on both sides. The focus of the relationship shifts from their problems to what they have together. Moreover, by being supportive of each other, they can help each other achieve great things in the future.

Sadness is a perfectly natural feeling and it's absolutely fine to feel sad and mourn for someone or something you have lost. But there is no benefit in sadness for a prolonged period of time.

When it comes to guilt, it's part of being human to make mistakes. The important thing is to learn from your mistakes, show contrition to anyone that you've hurt and make sure that you don't make the same mistake again.

By holding on to the negative things from our past we rob ourselves of the energy we need to live the life of our dreams.

Don't dwell on the past, because it doesn't really matter where you have been. What counts is where you're going.

While none of us can escape from our past, by learning from it and letting go of it we can actually use it to help create a much better future.

For one who has conquered the mind, the mind is the best of friends. But for one who has failed to do so, his very mind will be his greatest enemy.
Bhagavad Gita

MIND, SET & MATCH

Anyway

People are often unreasonable, illogical
And self centred.
Forgive them anyway.

If you are kind, people may accuse you
Of selfish, ulterior motives;
Be kind anyway.

If you are successful, you will win some
False friends and some true enemies;
Succeed anyway.

If you are honest and frank,
People may cheat you;
Be honest and frank anyway.

What you spend years building, someone
Could destroy overnight;
Build anyway.

If you find serenity and happiness,
They may be jealous;
Be happy anyway.

The good you do today,
People will often forget tomorrow;
Do good anyway.

Give the world the best you have,
And it may never be enough;
Give the world the best you've got anyway.

You see, in the final analysis,
It is between you and God;
It was never between you and them anyway.

Anon. (found on the wall of Mother Teresa's office)

**We are what we think. All that we are arises with our thoughts.
With our thoughts we make the world.**
Buddha

"How Do You Do That?"

As a psychotherapist I've worked with many depressed people.

In the first therapy session I always ask them, "How do you do that? How do you manage to stay depressed? It's amazing – can you teach me how you do it?"

The initial reaction is usually one of bewilderment. They then go on to explain that their thinking is very black and white, that they dwell on negative thoughts to the total exclusion of everything else, and always expect the worst to happen.

"So," I say, "it seems to me that you actually get what you think about all the time. Would you agree?" Invariably they do.

Next I ask, "What do you think might happen if you think about positive things with the same intensity and focus that you do about negative things? What do you think might happen then?"

To get the results that we want in life, we need to follow the same process as depressed people do, but dwell on positive and not negative thoughts. People who are consistently happy consistently think positive thoughts.

So choose carefully what thoughts enter your mind. Remember that your mind is sacred and only those thoughts that are of direct benefit to you should be allowed to enter.

Those who really seek the path to enlightenment dictate terms to their mind. They then proceed with strong determination.

Buddha

MIND, SET & MATCH

If negative thoughts are about to enter your head, then act as if you have a firewall or anti-virus software in your brain. Stop them at source before they start to mess up your mind.

One of the parents at my kid's school runs a martial arts centre and has trained at the world famous Shaolin School in China.

We got talking about some of the remarkable feats that the monks from the school can achieve. Recent research by a group of Chinese neurologists shows that by using only 1 to 3% more of their brain, the Shaolin monks are able to perform amazing exploits such as resting their whole body weight on the point of a razor-sharp spear, and bending thick iron bars by being hit on the head with them. They attribute this to their ability to control their thoughts and focus on their inner energy, or *chi*.

If you can harness the power of the mind you can achieve anything. The only thing stopping you from achieving the results you want is the quality of your thinking.

As a man thinketh in his heart, so is he.
Proverbs 23:7

Starve the Monkey

Negative thoughts and limiting beliefs wither away when they receive no attention. By entertaining them you nourish them and keep them alive. When you don't think about them they die.

The more the mind is occupied by challenging and rewarding tasks, the less room there is for negative thoughts and feelings. Why do you think some people throw themselves into their work after the loss of a loved one?

The human mind cannot think two thoughts at the same time. By focusing your thoughts on your vision and immersing yourself in the right actions, you starve the monkey on your back to death.

Any negative thoughts or images that are part of our self-talk need attention in order to survive. As long as we focus on realising our desires, our negative self-talk will cease.

An old man was talking to his grandson, who was angry at a schoolmate who had done him an injustice. The old man said, "Let me tell you a story. I've struggled with these feelings many times.

"I too have felt a great hate for those who have hurt me, with no sorrow for what they have done. But hate wears you down, and doesn't hurt your enemy. It's like taking poison and wishing your enemy would die.

"It's as if there are two monkeys on my shoulder. One is good

Man is what he believes.
Anton Chekhov

and does no harm. He lives in harmony with all those around him and doesn't take offence when none was intended. He'll only fight when it's right to do so, and in the right way.

"But the other monkey, ah! He is full of anger. The smallest thing will set him off. He fights everyone, all the time, for no reason. He can't think because his anger and hate are so great. It's hard to live with these two monkeys, for both of them try to dominate my spirit."

The boy looked intently into his grandfather's eye and asked, "Which one wins, Grandad?"

The old man solemnly replied, "The one I feed."

Nurture your minds with great thoughts.
To believe in the heroic makes heroes.
Benjamin Disraeli

You Get What You Expect, Not What You Want

Your expectations determine what you will do. The whole effort of realising your dream lies in converting your 'can' into 'will'. Expectation is the mental environment in which your talents are either nurtured or repressed. You can no more change your innate talents than the colour of your eyes, but you can change your expectations.

Be clear about what you want, and then have faith that it will come. You should prepare for good things and expect them to happen. Act prosperously in real life. Life has a way of shaping itself to our expectations, good or bad, so let your thoughts and actions express relaxed, unwavering faith.

Whether you're looking for a lost set of keys, a parking space, or the kind of work you love, expecting to find it makes all the difference. It allows you to relax, stay focused on your objectives and move towards them. It reduces the sense of impatience and frustration that might cause you to give up. While we all encounter obstacles on the way to our dreams, those who expect to succeed persevere long after others have given up.

You get what you expect, so you should expect the best. When what we want conflicts with what we expect, we get what we expect, not what we want.

Expect that you will. Believe in your destiny.

They can because they think they can.
Virgil

MIND, SET & MATCH

Victor Wolfenstein, a professor at UCLA, has extensively studied the lives of those considered the 'greats' of history. He has found that time and time again these people have an innate sense of destiny about them. People like Gandhi, Lenin, Napoleon and, more recently, Barack Obama.

They all believed that they would ultimately succeed. That belief sustained them through dark periods when, by all appearance, they had no right or reason to believe they would prevail. It is low expectations, more than any lack of talent, character flaw or external barrier which keeps us from realising our full potential.

Studies have been conducted to discover if there are any identifiable environmental or genetic characteristics that can be linked to creativity. Researchers looked at IQ, social and economic background, education, and a number of other variables.

The only factor that was found in any way to correlate with creativity, as measured by the researchers, was the individual's belief that he or she was creative. People who believe they are creative actually are more so. Even if you have doubts, claim your creativity and watch it grow.

Studies tell us that people learn and perform far better in the face of encouragement and the expectation of success than they do under constant belittlement. You foster self-belief in people by changing your expectations of them. Tests show that pupils tend to perform as well as their teachers and

Whether you think you can or you can't, you are right.
Henry Ford

parents expect them to. In the same way, employees generally perform up to the level that their bosses and their peers expect of them.

In the course of our upbringing, many of us became accustomed to settling for less. Habituated to low expectations and saddled with a negative self-image, we never entertain the idea that we could, should, or would accomplish anything great.

While our limiting beliefs are a result of our upbringing, it's useless to wish we had been raised differently. The better course is to raise yourself to a new level of expectation.

Napoleon Hill, author of the classic motivational book *Think And Grow Rich*, grew up in abject poverty. He recognised that his upbringing had programmed him with a poverty mindset. He knew that unless he deliberately intervened and changed his thought processes, his fate was sealed. Since he had already been conditioned to expect a life of poverty, he knew it was up to him to change his mindset and live by a different standard. He understood that in order to raise the level of our achievements, we first have to raise our expectations.

You give birth to that which you fix your mind.
Antoine de Saint-Exupéry

The World's Biggest Club

Fear knocked at the door
Faith answered
There was no-one there
Anon.

Fear is our greatest enemy. Nothing of any note can be achieved without confronting and mastering fear.

Negative emotions, including anger, sadness and guilt, are born of fear and/or attachment. By letting go of fear and becoming detached, we need suffer no longer. It's when we're not crippled by fear that we can play the game of life, rather than letting life play with us.

Any fear that we have has been learned from our environment. We weren't born with fear. The good news is that we can unlearn this fear.

Dr Martin Seligman of the University of Pennsylvania, a leading expert in the field of positive psychology, has concluded following extensive research that as much as 80% of the adult population has a feeling of learned helplessness. Once you realise that your mind is unlimited and that everything is possible, you lose the fear that cripples you.

I've coached many people who have been on the path to success and then suddenly self-sabotage. They do this because they are afraid of failure.

**This time like all times, is a very good one,
if we but know what to do with it.**
Ralph Waldo Emerson

THOUGHTS BECOME REALITY

If your vision is precious to you, but ultimately you don't try to manifest it, you can always seek comfort in the knowledge that you didn't fail. A phrase that I nearly always hear these self-sabotagers say is "I would have – if only…"

There is absolutely no merit or reward in joining the world's biggest club:

The "If Only" club.

The happiness of your life depends on the quality of your thoughts.
Marcus Aurelius

Unlimited Potential

Unfortunately millions of people sell themselves short because they believe there is nothing they can do to change their lot. This simply isn't true. As Napoleon Hill said, "Whatever the mind of man can conceive and believe, it can achieve."

We limit ourselves with limiting thoughts and self-defeating behaviours.

Your potential is quite simply unlimited. Since your thoughts create your reality, and you're free to choose your thoughts, you are therefore only limited by the quality of your thinking.

Much of the difference between failure and success lies in what you believe you're entitled to do. So you may as well think big.

You become what you think about most of the time. If you think that you're a very happy person who is valued by his fellow man, then that is what you will become.

The first and most critical step towards getting the life that you want is to take complete responsibility for your life now, and accept that YOU are responsible for creating your reality. If there are areas of your life that you're not entirely happy with, don't attribute these to poor circumstances or bad luck, because you have helped to create the situation by the quality of your thinking.

If you are going to let poverty govern your life, your reward will be that you will eat, but you will not live.
George Bernard Shaw

THOUGHTS BECOME REALITY

Once you take responsibility for your life, it's empowering to know that you are totally in control of your own life; not anyone or anything else.

Accept your present situation, good, bad or indifferent, because it's where you need to be for your own personal growth and development to begin.

As Aristotle said in his *Metaphysics*, there is a universal principle of causality. Everything happens for a reason because we live in a universe where all events have a cause-effect relationship. Just because you don't know why something has happened, it does not mean that there is no reason for it.

Success is nothing more than a few simple disciplines practised every day.
Jim Rohn

The Power of Now

Extensive research has shown that successful people, whether they be in business, sport, the arts or any other walk of life, share one common trait: they are all excellent at staying in the moment.

They don't worry about what they haven't got or what they aren't able to do. It's not about what they cannot do, rather it's about what they can do now with what they have got.

Successful entrepreneurs don't spend lots of time deciding on how they are going to be successful. They are very good at living in the now and taking action.

One of my favourite fashion designers is Sir Paul Smith, the owner of a retail business worth nearly half a billion dollars. He was asked by a journalist what advice he would give individuals seeking to replicate his success. He replied, "Life isn't about working shorter or longer hours. It's about every hour. It's about every minute and every second. Learn to live in the moment."

The present moment represents your point of power. It's by taking action in the present moment that you create your future.

Change is not merely necessary to life, it is life.
Alvin Toffler

Detached Engagement

Work like you don't need money
Love like you've never been hurt,
And dance like no one's watching
Mark Twain

All the stress in your life results from your fixed notion of how the universe should behave. However, the universe is not obliged to follow your agenda. The temptation is to take any departures from your script as a personal affront.

All of us want the people in our lives – partners, parents, children, siblings, relatives, friends, neighbours, bosses and colleagues – to behave in particular ways that we determine. But they often don't conform to what we want.

Just think of the amount of time and energy that can be wasted trying to 'fix' these people. It's stressful getting angry with people, pleading with them, threatening them, cajoling them, explaining to them. No wonder you feel stressed.

The only way you can prevent toxic feelings being generated inside yourself is to accept whatever outcome actually occurs.

Surrender to the universe. Remember that the stress in your life is caused by your reaction to not getting what you want. You can eliminate all this stress by surrendering. When you do this, probably more than 90% of the stress you were experiencing will simply disappear. Just like that. It will leave your life and the relief you feel will be palpable and immediate.

**Do not wait for life. Be aware at every moment
that the miracle is in the here and now.**
Marcel Proust

Detachment, like any other skill, is something that can be practised. The more you practise it, the better you get.

With practice it will soon seem the universe is collaborating with you, instead of thwarting you at every turn. And it is. It's as if the two of you are locked together in an intimate dance. And you are. When you realise this, your life will never be the same again.

It may well take time before you see this happening routinely in your life. It doesn't matter. You will, quite quickly, see enough instances of this happening to gain the confidence that more and more of it can happen. Persist patiently and you cannot fail.

As the tennis coach Timothy Gallwey said, "Your body is smarter than you think: trust it to achieve the goals you have set. The secret to winning any game is in not trying too hard."

Uncluttered with words and instructions, a still mind makes for the best performance.

I'm a big tennis fan and was fortunate enough to see John McEnroe beat Jimmy Connors 6-1 6-1 6-2 to win the 1984 Wimbledon title. The veteran commentator Dan Maskell described McEnroe's performance as the greatest grass court tennis ever played.

After the match, McEnroe was asked what he was thinking when he hit a miraculous cross-court volley off his shoelaces after a blistering service return from Connors. After a pause

**Obstacles don't make people stop –
people stop themselves.**
Carol Quinn

THOUGHTS BECOME REALITY

to think, McEnroe replied, "Nothing." This is because he was so in the moment, playing the game at the subconscious level. He was in tune with the universe.

When Goran Ivanesevic beat Pat Rafter in the 2001 Wimbledon final he did it on his fourth match point. He was asked what his emotions were during those match points. "On the first three match points I knew that I was just one serve away from achieving my dream. I was so nervous I could hardly lift up the racket. It felt like it weighed 40kgs. On the fourth match point, I just concentrated on the serve and forgetting that I was serving to be Wimbledon champion."

Once you have given an emotional meaning to an event, you are less able to be fully aware of the next moment because you are caught up in the emotion.

Success comes when you temporarily withhold thoughts and emotions of success or failure and stay in the present. Without such distractions you can be calmly effective. To play at your best, you must live every second in the present. This is real concentration: all your energies are focused on this one moment, this one point.

Through not being attached to the fruits of victory, you paradoxically become free to play the game for itself in a more relaxed and powerful state of mind. Through non-attachment, winning becomes more likely.

Track athletes try to stay loose and relaxed at all times, but

If you're not enjoying the journey, you probably won't enjoy the destination.

Joe Tye

especially when they're in the home straight and the lactic acid building up in their muscles makes them start to tighten and slow down You often hear a sports commentator use the phrase "he tightened up" to indicate the reason behind a poor performance. The more you try to force something to happen, the less likely you are to achieve it.

The saddest words of tongue or pen are these four words – it might have been.
Oliver Wendell Holmes

If

If you can keep your head when all about you
Are losing theirs and blaming it on you;
If you can trust yourself when all men doubt you,
But make allowance for their doubting too;

If you can wait and not be tired by waiting,
Or, being lied about, don't deal in lies,
Or, being hated, don't give way to hating,
And yet don't look too good, nor talk too wise;

If you can dream – and not make dreams your
master;
If you can think – and not make thoughts your aim;
If you can meet with triumph and disaster
And treat those two impostors just the same;

If you can bear to hear the truth you've spoken
Twisted by knaves to make a trap for fools,
Or watch the things you gave your life to broken,
And stoop and build 'em up with worn-out tools;

If you can make one heap of all your winnings
And risk it on one turn of pitch-and-toss,
And lose, and start again at your beginnings
And never breathe a word about your loss;

**Either we have our dreams or we
live our dreams.**
Zoe Koplowitz

MIND, SET & MATCH

If you can force your heart and nerve and sinew
To serve your turn long after they are gone,
And so hold on when there is nothing in you
Except the will which says to them, "Hold on";

If you can talk with crowds and keep your virtue,
Or walk with kings nor lose the common touch;
If neither foes nor loving friends can hurt you;
If all men count with you, but none too much;

If you can fill the unforgiving minute
With sixty seconds' worth of distance run,
Yours is the Earth and everything that's in it,
And – which is more – you'll be a man, my son!

Rudyard Kipling

**To find an open road, have an
open mind.**
John Towne

The Subconscious Mind

When you understand the relationship between the conscious and the subconscious mind, you'll understand the power of belief.

The subconscious continually works to express our deepest beliefs and passions. Because the subconscious operates in terms of imagery, it's vital that we feed it mental pictures of what we desire. It can then go to work on living up to the image placed before it by giving us intuitions about what to do, where to go, and who to meet.

The subconscious is connected to all other parts of our mind, and can attract events and people to us that will assist in making our dreams a reality.

However, it will only find ways to turn the imagery into reality if the images are clear and convincing; hence the importance of the mental pictures of success that we feed it. The force of belief can't work in our favour until the belief literally becomes part of us, settled in the subconscious mind as a fact.

The thoughts you hold about yourself are effectively beamed out to the world through your subconscious, boomeranging back to you as your circumstances.

If you have belief, if you have a positive mental attitude, it's amazing what hardships you can overcome and what you can achieve.

**We cannot become what we want to be
by remaining what we are.**
Max Dupree

MIND, SET & MATCH

Optimism is power because it energises you, and your expectation resonates with the universe.

One of the greatest examples of triumph over adversity is Nelson Mandela. No matter what happened to him, Mandela believed that one day he would be freed from prison and lead his people into peace. Despite spending 27 years in jail, that's exactly what he did. Most other men would have become resigned to their fate and remained on Robben Island until they died.

Can anything be sadder than work unfinished?
Yes, work never begun.
Christina Rossetti

Movies of the Mind

All the leading sportsmen and women, people like Tiger Woods and Serena Williams, use a sports psychologist to improve their performance by using mental techniques such as visualisation, relaxation and positive affirmations.

Whenever you visualise yourself performing in sports, electromyographical (EMG) activity in the musculature increases and primes the muscles to perform at the level you are visualising.

Once your mind has visualised a positive outcome your newly improved focus will begin to work alongside your automatic responses in a better, more flowing manner and your determination will increase along with the confidence in your ability. This is what increases performance levels and standards.

The more control a sportsman or woman has over their imagination, the greater the outcome they can achieve. Psychologists have now found that these mental techniques can be successfully used in daily life, so all of us can learn how to think like champions.

The principles of the psychology of peak performance can be applied throughout your life. Anyone who wants to enhance their performance – be it on the playing field, in the boardroom or in the bedroom – needs to think about their mental approach.

We think caged birds sing, when indeed they cry.
John Webster

It's not so much about 'psyching out' your opposition as 'psyching up' yourself.

Studies have shown that up to 70% of our thoughts are negative in nature. Visualisation and positive affirmations help to replace those negative thoughts with positive concentration.

I was at a wedding recently and met a very likeable chap called David, who gave me a very detailed account of what his dream house looks like. He told me it had a long circular drive with triple garage, black granite worktops in the solid oak kitchen, a cinema room with the very latest TV and entertainment system, a fitness centre complete with swimming pool, and so on. He then proceeded to tell me that he would never have such a house because it was far too big a leap from his present circumstances.

While his vision is clear, David's thoughts and language make it impossible to realise this vision. He doesn't truly believe that he'll get this house as he can't see past his present circumstances. Since his dominant thought is that he will never acquire his dream house, then the universe is delivering exactly that!!

Be very careful about your fears, as you get what you imagine most clearly – both good and bad. How many times have you heard people say, "I was afraid that would happen."

If you want that dream house, then focus your thoughts as if you are 100% certain you will get it. Be in a state of

If we always do what we always did, we will always get what we always got.
Jackie Mabley

heightened expectation, knowing that the house is yours. Know that your asking has been answered. Plan the move in detail, identify the removals firm, decorators, the house warming party, the invitation list, what food and drink will you provide, what you will say when raising a toast, how you will feel at the party.

Visualise as much detail as possible. What can you see, hear, feel and smell? Remember, the stronger the desire and expectation, the quicker your desires will be delivered.

Go beyond the dream as if it has already happened. Visualise how it has changed your life. What do you do with your day, now that you have realised your dream and your circumstances are so different?

Book time with yourself, especially first thing in the morning and before you go to bed, to look at your goals and visualise their fulfilment. Try to do this during the day as well. It may only take a few minutes on each occasion.

If you do this, synchronicity will occur. The intensity of your emotions is essential: the more emotional you are, the stronger the signal that you send to the universe and the more quickly things will happen. This emotion actually fuels your dream coming true.

As you do your visualisation day after day you'll notice that more and more synchronicities happen. Do your visualisations once in the morning and once before you go

The world is your world. Take it easy, but take it.
Woody Guthrie

to bed, but don't try too hard and make sure that you remain detached from the outcome. Five to ten minutes a day is more than enough.

Visualising longer than that each day is counter-productive, because you'll find it difficult not to daydream and also maintain the intensity of the emotions.

Make sure that you're in the picture when you visualise and are in your body looking through your own eyes, as opposed to seeing yourself in the picture. Again, this makes your visualisation very real.

When you visualise, always focus on the end result, not how the result is going to come about. If you focus on the process, you're actually limiting the number of ways your dreams can come true. Don't limit yourself to one possibility. There are likely to be millions of ways that your dreams may come true.

For example, if you're looking for the perfect relationship the traditional route might be via dating agencies. Why restrict your visualisation to this one channel when there are so many other ways to meet? You might bump into your soul mate while out shopping, or parking your car, or walking down the street, or at work, or on holiday, or at a party, or at a wedding or in a restaurant… The list goes on and on. There are so many people and so many ways to meet and fall in love. Focus on taking the action that you need to take, and leave the 'how' to the universe.

You're only given a little spark of madness. You mustn't lose it.
Robin Williams

THOUGHTS BECOME REALITY

There must be no inconsistencies in your mind, as the subconscious mind will only create a reality which you wholeheartedly believe and desire.

Believe with every cell in your body that you're successful and radiate this abundance to others, for nothing succeeds like the appearance of success. People want to be around inspirational people, and you're helping them by allowing your light to shine.

**Having fun is not a diversion from a
successful life; it is the pathway to it.**
Martha Beck

Positive Affirmations

To explain the value of positive affirmations, the sports psychologist Trevor Dodd tells the story of a tennis player whose form slumped soon after tie breaks were introduced to the game.

"This player was in the world's top 50 but he just couldn't win a tie break. It was driving him mad with anxiety and as a result he lost seven tie breaks – and seven matches – in a row. He realised that there was no point in competing at an international level unless he could beat his *bête noire*."

"I taught him to brainwash himself in reverse cycle – into believing he could play tie breaks.

"He did this by convincing himself, when he was in relaxed situations, that he loved tie breaks. He stuck notes saying 'I love tie breaks' on his bathroom mirror so that they greeted him first thing in the morning. He repeated 'I love tie breaks' over and over to himself throughout the day and scrawled this mantra on whatever paper he could find, even on serviettes in restaurants. He won nine of the next eleven tie breaks that he played."

This player went from a strong belief that he would fail and a success rate of 0%, to believing that he loved tie breaks and a success rate of over 80%. He achieved this complete turnaround by quite simply programming his mind to believe what he wanted.

**No one can make you feel inferior
without your consent.**
Eleanor Roosevelt

Clean Language

Thoughts create our reality and actions, and words come from our thoughts.

If we knew for an absolute certainty that our words create our reality, then we would be very, very careful about what we say. We would use what psychologists call 'clean language'.

Clean language is language that doesn't contain any negative thoughts and emotions. Phrases such as "I'm poor, life is so hard, life isn't fair, I'm unlucky" would all be consigned to the dustbin and never uttered again if we knew for absolute certainty that our words, because they are spoken thoughts, create our reality.

What we say becomes a self-fulfilling prophecy. A client of mine, Sam, is a classic example of this. Before he went on holiday Sam told me, "Something always goes wrong when I go on holiday. I'm just waiting for something bad to happen." Sure enough, when he got to the airport he discovered that one of the passports was out of date. Fortunately it was a young child's passport and he was allowed to travel. Sam was in the same negative frame of mind when he arrived in the south of France and phoned me to say he had left the key to the villa back home on the kitchen table. Then he hired a car and it had a flat tyre.

It's worth repeating: the universe doesn't differentiate between negative and positive thinking. It will deliver your thinking

> **Caring is the ultimate competitive advantage.**
> Ron Kendrick

MIND, SET & MATCH

regardless of whether it's negative or positive – hence Sam's negative thinking came true.

When he came back from holiday we sat down and I said to him, "You've got to think more positively." I explained that our thoughts create our reality and the penny seemed to drop. The next day was Monday and Sam came home from work much earlier than usual. He had just been made redundant – for the fourth time in seven years.

It quickly became clear that Sam didn't really like what he was doing anyway. He felt he had far more talent than the job required. He told me that while he enjoyed working in the corporate environment, he would prefer working as a freelance so that he didn't get involved in office politics. He preferred to focus on what he did best, designing and developing software systems to measure productivity and risk.

As I started to explore Sam's thinking and belief systems, it became apparent that while on the surface he was a very positive, bubbly, effervescent character, when it came to work and money his thinking and his belief systems were negative and he actually dwelled in poverty consciousness. He had a great marriage, two lovely kids and fabulous friends. His language patterns in these areas of his life were fantastic. He used superlatives like "great", "fabulous", "awesome", "brilliant".

The worst fear is the fear of living.
Theodore Roosevelt

THOUGHTS BECOME REALITY

In order to move towards a mindset of wealth consciousness we composed some positive affirmations that Sam was comfortable with, and set a goal that he would go seven days without thinking a negative thought about money. If he did have a negative money thought in that period, the clock was reset to zero and he would have to start again. Although it took him two months to achieve the 'seven consecutive days' target, things started to change within a couple of weeks.

Within three months Sam had attended a series of interviews which resulted in him accepting a lucrative contract with a major broadcaster, effectively doubling his salary.

Try the seven day challenge. It's one of the most powerful exercises I know to create a winner's mindset.

If you think positive thoughts and say only those things which serve and support you, you may be surprised how quickly your thoughts come true.

No one rises to low expectations.
Les Brown

Blue Trees

Frame your thinking about what your heart desires in positive, not negative, terms. For example, "I want to be healthy" rather than "I don't want to be fat", or "I want to be financially secure" rather than "I don't want to be poor".

If your thinking is "away from" as opposed to "towards", you will be reactive as opposed to proactive. You will think about (not) being fat and (not) being poor, and inevitably images of fatness and poverty will shape your thoughts – the very images you need to avoid.

If I say to you, "Don't think of a blue tree", you will have to picture a blue tree in order to know what to avoid!

And given that you get what you think about, you really don't want to be holding negative images of being poor or being fat. Moreover, these images don't energise you, they won't fill you with positive expectation, or nourish the belief that's required for you to manifest your desires.

Trust yourself, you know far more than you think you do.
Dr. Benjamin Spock

Capital without Punishment

If you dwell in poverty consciousness and believe that you'll never be wealthy, that's the quickest way to ensure that money does not come your way. Remove your limiting beliefs about money by not focusing on them. If the old negative thoughts keep popping up, ask yourself what benefit you derive from holding on to them.

If, on the other hand, you dwell in wealth consciousness and believe that you are wealthy, then this is the quickest way to become wealthy. If you want a new car or house then start looking for one and believe that you can have whatever you want. Believe that you have a very healthy bank balance and reinforce this belief by using positive affirmations. You'll be amazed how synchronistic events and serendipity will conspire to deliver what you want.

The first step towards increasing your wealth is to take responsibility for your financial situation. Know that you can easily improve it by changing your perception about money.

There's no value to anyone, not least yourself, in being a martyr when it comes to money. You can't help the poor by becoming one of them. True wealth is about being happy, not having lots of cash. But few people will argue that having money helps to make life easier.

I come across many people who tell me that money is not important to them. Virtually all these people don't have as

When you have confidence, you can have a lot of fun. And when you have fun, you can do amazing things.
Joe Namath

much money as they would genuinely like. They don't have any aspirations in this area for fear of failure, or being labelled a failure by others.

Accumulating money for its own sake is not a good idea – 'miser' and 'misery' are too close for comfort – but the ability to prosper by giving value to others has a lot to be said for it.

Material wealth and spiritual growth are not incompatible. There's no virtue in being poor; not only do you radiate poverty rather than abundance, but you are also in no position to help anyone else. The more you have, the more you can enjoy and share with other people.

Keep the money flowing, use it wisely, enjoy it, save some, but don't hoard it and become like a stagnant pond. It's by using money and keeping it flowing that we attract more.

Consistently saving a proportion of your income creates a financial reserve which will give you more confidence to be your authentic self and take a few risks. People who become wealthy have usually taken a risk or two along the way.

Trust that by being your authentic self, and being of service, you will always have what you desire. Always ensure that you're making a contribution to the quality of other people's lives. Don't get caught up in the belief that you have to work twelve hours a day every day to become wealthy. I've never come across a wealthy person yet who has relied on his hourly rate.

Bury your ego. Don't be the star.
Be the star maker.
Bud Hadfield

THOUGHTS BECOME REALITY

Money in itself has no value; it's an abstraction of work. How well you are rewarded for your efforts is directly proportional to the results that you achieve for other people. The greater these results and the quicker that you can achieve them for other people, the greater your reward.

Charge for your services according to the value that you add. I was once on the verge of winning a large piece of business but the client was reluctant to pay my fee. I asked him if he believed in my capabilities and also my ability to deliver what I had promised. He said he did not doubt either.

I then reframed the situation by asking him what it would be worth to him to have the current problem solved. He replied "I'm not sure exactly, but probably over a million pounds." He then looked at me with a smile and signed the contract.

Learn from others who have become wealthy and immerse yourself in stories of success and the literature of positive psychology. By doing so you'll be further inspired to achieve your dreams, and realise that you really can think yourself rich.

Be grateful every day for what you have. I have yet to meet a wealthy, happy person who is not grateful for the abundance in their life. This simple act of gratitude will attract more money into your life.

**As we grow older, we discover that we have two hands.
One for helping ourselves, the second for helping others.**
Unknown

Personal Mastery

What you believe about yourself, the world will believe about you.

You create your world from what's inside you, so you need to go within yourself. Otherwise you will go without.

The way to real personal mastery is to sweep away those beliefs and thought patterns that block the energy you require to manifest your desires, and replace them with beliefs and thought patterns which inspire you to take the right action.

Greater awareness will melt away your current patterns of thinking and allow you to install new thought patterns which have the power to change your life.

Awareness is the only tool you'll ever need to create the life of your dreams.

Awareness makes you pause and think about what you're letting into your mental DNA. Gradually you get to the point where you can control what you let into your mind. It's when you increase your level of self-awareness that your life starts to straighten out and you begin to follow the path that you want.

Every great thing starts with a thought, and is powered into realisation by a belief. There's a golden thread that runs through all religions and esoteric teachings: the power of belief is limitless.

**He who wants to do good knocks at the gate;
he who loves opens the gate.**
Tagore

THOUGHTS BECOME REALITY

The technique of thought repetition first overcomes reason by acting on our emotions and then penetrates into the subconscious, where it is only a matter of time before the thought is enacted. This is the principle behind successful advertising. When you've learned how to draw on your subconscious powers, there is really no limit to what you can accomplish.

The majority of people who fail in life are simply the victims of their own mental defeats. Individuals who settle for mediocrity do so because they don't really believe in themselves.

Just as a magnet can lift a metal object ten times its size or more, so a highly magnetised person, charged with confidence and purpose, can do at least ten times more than someone who is not so energised.

If you're not getting the results that you want, you might think your train has come off its tracks - it hasn't. It's just that you're probably on the wrong track and you simply need to change. The track you're on might be leading nowhere, but learn from the experience. You'll have learnt some invaluable lessons which will help you to change to the right track and start to move forward.

The only reason that you're not where you want to be, is that your current reality is the product of your previous thoughts.

The only thing separating you today, from the life of your

If a man does not keep pace with his companions perhaps it is because he hears a different drummer. Let him step to the music he hears.
Henry David Thoreau

dreams tomorrow, is the thoughts you think between here and there. If you were to remember only one thing from this book, then it should be that your thoughts become your reality.

If you keep thinking the same thought it will become a belief and eventually materialise before your very eyes.

Your thoughts today are a preview of what you will manifest tomorrow. You can be, do or have anything you want to if you think the right thoughts and do the right things. It's by thinking the right thoughts that you'll be doing the right things, because it's your thinking that drives your beliefs, your values and the actions that you take.

As a psychotherapist I've worked with many people who think that they have to endure or cope with their personal situation. They simply don't believe that everyone has the choice to solve their problems and be completely free of them.

Beliefs really can change instantaneously if you allow them to. Once your beliefs have changed and are in tune with your vision, you'll start to see a change in your reality.

If you're holding onto a belief that doesn't help you, examine why you're holding on to it. Be sure to get to the root cause. For example, I was coaching a client who believed that he could never maintain his ideal weight. This was based on an early childhood memory when his grandmother said to him, "Your mum and dad are both overweight so you will be too."

For every minute that you are angry you lose sixty seconds worth of happiness.
Ralph Waldo Emerson

We then identified that his mother and father had no underlying health problems and there was no medical reason why they couldn't lose weight. They simply ate too much of the wrong food and took no exercise.

The old belief was dislodged and replaced by a new one – that being healthy and trim was a perfectly natural state of affairs.

The result? My client went on to maintain his ideal weight easily.

If you're finding that you're not getting the change that you want in a particular area of your life, ask yourself what you are gaining by holding on to a belief which doesn't support you? What would happen to you if you let go of it?

Do the maths:

$$\text{Event} + \text{Response} = \text{Outcome}$$

If E and R are constant, then O will always be the same.

In other words, if you keep on doing what you're doing then you'll keep on getting what you're getting. It's strange, but so many people think that by repeating the same behaviour over and over again, they'll achieve a different result. You need to change the way that you respond to events in order to get the outcome that you're looking for.

You have created your reality through the choices that you've made and the thoughts and emotions that you attach to each

Don't let what you cannot do interfere with what you can do.
John Wooden

MIND, SET & MATCH

event. If you change the way that you perceive events, then you'll change your response to them and achieve a different result.

Activity and sadness are incompatible.
Christian Bovee

CHAPTER 4

SET YOURSELF ON FIRE

How to Love Mondays

Do you enjoy your work, or is it a struggle? How do you feel when Monday morning comes around and it's time to go back to work?

The potential in people is enormous but usually remains dormant because their work doesn't reconcile with who they are and their innate purpose.

Everyone was put on this planet for a purpose. We all have a unique role to play. Each of us must find our own path and celebrate our unique gifts and abilities. Once we've found what we love to do and give ourselves to it wholeheartedly, happiness and abundance will inevitably follow.

When you're inspired and driven by purpose, your mind will break all boundaries and your consciousness will expand. Your creativity and talent will flow and you'll discover that you're a greater person than you ever dreamed yourself to be.

You need to put to one side the 'should's and the 'could's and listen to your heart. Listen to your intuition and do what you were born to do. If you listen to and trust your heart you'll not go far wrong in life.

Imagine that you've been given £20m by your fairy godmother, but only on condition that you can't give any away to family or friends. Before vanishing, your fairy godmother tells you that she has also granted you eternal life. What would you do

> **Without work, all life goes rotten. But when work is soulless, life stifles and dies.**
> Albert Camus

with your life? The answer to this question may well be your legacy in real life. Ask yourself whether you are on the right path to achieve it.

Whatever your life's purpose, it will ultimately include being creative in some way, because to grow is to create. Our innermost desires are to learn, grow and be happy.

The brain is wired to promote survival. In fact, the brain will reward the body for things it recognises as necessary to survive. By solving problems, humans are better placed to survive and overcome changes in their environment. We are problem-solving creatures.

One of the most ingenious characteristics of the brain is its reward system. When we solve problems, overcome challenges or achieve something which stretches us, the brain rewards us. The chemical dopamine is released which causes feelings of euphoria as a positive reinforcement for the behaviour. Think of it as giving a dog a treat when it sits on command. Your brain gives your body a treat when you engage in a behaviour the brain recognises as important.

For a moment cast aside the baggage of conditioning. Ask yourself, what would you do if you knew you couldn't fail and would be paid what you wanted?

You can do whatever you want.

The choice has always been yours.

Whatever you do, or dream you can do – begin it.
Boldness has genius, power and magic in it.
Goethe

Your purpose and that of every other human being is to express your true self. If you listen to your heart and intuition and act accordingly, then you will affirm who you are.

The more you do who you are, the better you will do. Not only will this set you free, but you will also inspire others to break free. As Marianne Williamson said in *A Return to Love: Reflections on the Principles of A Course in Miracles*:

> "Our deepest fear is not that we are inadequate. Our deepest fear is that we are powerful beyond measure. It is our light, not our darkness that most frightens us.

> "We ask ourselves, 'Who am I to be brilliant, gorgeous, talented, fabulous?' Actually, who are you not to be? You are a child of God. Your playing small does not serve the world. There is nothing enlightened about shrinking so that other people won't feel insecure around you. We are all meant to shine, as children do. We were born to make manifest the glory of God that is within us. It's not just in some of us; it's in everyone. And as we let our own light shine, we unconsciously give other people permission to do the same. As we are liberated from our own fear, our presence automatically liberates others."

You imagine what you desire; you will what you imagine, and at last you create what you will.
George Bernard Shaw

We can be interested in many things, but only really dedicated to a few. Excellence is a matter of dedication. Here then, is another great key to the discovery of your life's work: ask yourself, "What am I willing to dedicate myself to?"

Happiness is like a compass that indicates the path of life. You simply have to follow it, even though initially it may mean entering a way full of difficulties.

Only you know what you want to get out of life and what makes your heart dance. Answer the following questions spontaneously as if you were brainstorming:

- What are you truly passionate about?
- What would you do if you had access to all the resources you could possibly need?
- What would you do if you knew you couldn't fail?

The answers to these questions will lead you to discover your life's purpose. Do the things you love, and love the things you do. Pay attention to what excites you. Where your energy is, that's where your passion lies.

In order to love Mondays you have to:

- know who you really are
- transcend your ego, then express your unique talents
- realise that we're connected to everything else in the universe
- realise that love really does conquer all

Our plans miscarry because they have no aim. When a man does not know what harbour he is making for, no wind is the right wind.
Seneca

SET YOURSELF ON FIRE

Everyone has the ability to be excellent at something. This something is your unique gift to the world and it is in your heart. Just be still, empty your mind of all thought and let your heart guide you.

If you do this, Mondays will never be the same again.

If you refuse to accept anything but the best out of life, you very often get it.
Somerset Maugham

People Buy Passion

There is one thing in the world that you're definitely the best at. Not one person on the planet is better at this than you.

You're the very best at being yourself.

In a society where most things are in over-supply, the one thing that's extremely scarce is you.

In business, people are ultimately buying your passion for the product or service that you have to offer. That's why it's so much easier to sell something that you wholeheartedly believe in. Put yourself in everything that you do and in so doing you personalise your output – people will buy in to your uniqueness.

More than anything else, it's your passions that empower you to create and live the life of your dreams. The fire of creative passion burns brightly in every child, but as we get older many people find that they have forgotten to feed the fire and the flame has dimmed. What you need to do is stoke up that flame again and get the passion burning brightly. You fuel your passion by paying attention to what makes you feel alive and energised, to what interests and excites you.

Passion is more important than knowledge and effort. Only those who keep the fire of passion burning brightly have a chance of knowing what a truly wonderful thing it is to be alive. If you're going to live your passion, you must believe

To build the life you want, create the work you love.
Marsha Sinetar

that something inside of you is stronger than any outside circumstance.

Authentic people are like magnets and attract the people that they need. We crave authenticity. It's why so many people are hooked on reality TV. Whether they are house-mates or castaways, people being filmed 24 hours a day can't pretend for ever. Sooner or later they show their true colours. The more real and honest they are, the more we warm to them.

People will buy into you when you're just being who you are. When you're expressing your true self you'll be speaking directly to people's hearts and not just their heads.

This is when the real magic starts.

Undoubtedly, we become what we envisage.
Claude Bristol

Behind the Mask

Over the years I've worked with some very successful people who are key players in some of the world's leading companies. On the surface they seemed to have it all: high powered job, money to burn and all the trappings of wealth. However, when I got close to some of these people, I realised that they were hiding behind a mask of their own creation. Their success was based on less than solid foundations and was actually fuelled by deep-rooted feelings of inadequacy.

Particularly in corporate life, we're clever and smooth enough to fake it. Sure, you can do this for a while, even for years, but eventually we need to come out from behind the mask and express our true self. If we don't, we can never be truly happy; peace of mind will elude us and we will be far more prone to disease.

But we don't need to pretend to be someone else. We don't need to hide behind a mask and create a front that wins the approval of our paymasters.

By unlocking your passion and unleashing who you really are, the riches of the world are yours for the taking. It's only the expression of your authentic self that can lead to authentic happiness.

Never underestimate how far you can go by simply being yourself.

Where there is no vision, people perish.
Proverbs 29:18

The energy required to manifest your dreams comes from consistently expressing your authentic self. When you channel the emotional energy needed to keep up your mask into being who you really are, then you can achieve happiness and fulfilment as well as financial success.

Desire is possibility seeking expression.
Ralph Waldo Emerson

Be Selfish

It's essential that you're selfish. Don't choose work that only pays the mortgage. Keeping a steady job for the sake of the family may seem the sensible option, but it's really an excuse to stop you doing what you really want to.

By taking a chance and finding the flow of your work, you'll develop a passion and zest for life that will be infectious, particularly to your nearest and dearest. When you're in the flow, abundance will beat a path to your door. So by being selfish to get what you want, you actually get to give much more to your family, your friends and everyone who matters to you. Too many people fall into the trap of working to satisfy the expectations of others, usually parents, peers and employers.

The more time that you spend with the 'should's, the further you move away from your true self and the more dissatisfied and resentful you'll become.

I live the life of a professional speaker, author and coach not only because it makes me enormously happy and because I want to, but also because I have to. It's my purpose in life. It's what I do. If I don't live out my purpose, I'm going to be unhappy and have a negative impact on those around me.

Start a crusade in your life – to dare to be your best.
William Danforth

Man in the Mirror

When you get what you want in your struggle for self
And the world makes you king for the day,
Just go to a mirror and look at yourself
And see what that man has to say.

For it isn't your mother, or father, or wife
Whose judgment you must pass,
The fellow whose verdict counts most in your life
Is the one staring back from the glass.

Some people may think you're a straight-shooting chum
And call you a wonderful guy,
But the man in the glass says you're only a bum
If you can't look him straight in the eye.

He's the fellow to please, never mind all the rest,
For he is with you clear up to the end,
And you've passed your most dangerous, difficult test
If the man in the glass is your friend.

You may fool the whole world down the pathway of years,
And get pats on your back as you pass,
But your final reward will be heartache and tears,
If you're cheating the man in the glass.

Dale Wimbrow

**Not all birds can fly. What separates the flyers
from the walkers is the ability to take off.**
Carl Sagan

Latin Class

As a teenager I opted to study Latin, not because I was particularly interested in the language but because I loved the ancient stories in works such as Virgil's *Aeneid* and Horace's *Odes*.

It proved to be one of the better choices I made at school. Latin gives us the root of many of the words that we use today. By looking at how a word is derived, we can learn its deeper meaning.

For example, the word vocation is derived from the Latin word *vocare,* which literally means 'to call'. It's only when we become still, listen to our inner calling and take action that the universe will conspire positively to support us. Are you listening to your calling?

The word 'deserve' derives from two Latin words, *de* meaning 'from' and *servare* meaning 'to serve'. You only truly *deserve* something if it comes 'from service'.

The greater your service or value to others, the greater your rewards will be. So you really do get what you deserve.

On a recent birthday, I decided to go out with my wife and spoil myself with some retail therapy. It was the perfect autumn day: a cloudless blue sky, smiling sun gleaming through the red, yellow and orange leaves, an invigorating crispness in the air.

Nobody who ever gave his best regretted it.
George Halas

After a wonderful lunch and an exploratory stroll past various shop windows, it dawned on me that I didn't want to spend the rest of the afternoon indoors, searching for something that I really didn't need. So we decided to pick the kids up from school, go to the park and take a walk around the lake enjoying autumn's finest.

On my way back to the car I came across a store selling TAG sports watches, a brand which my best friend Sunny likes very much. At this point, I should mention that Sunny is one in a million. He is, quite simply, the most selfless, kind-hearted person that I have ever known. I suddenly thought what a great idea it would be to buy a watch for my dearest friend rather than spend the money on myself. My wife agreed wholeheartedly and the watch was purchased.

That evening when Sunny and a few other friends came to my house for a birthday dinner party, at the end of the meal I proudly announced, "I've one more present, but it's not for me. In our midst sits someone who sets the very highest standard when it comes to being kind, helpful, generous and completely selfless. I for one am humbled and truly privileged to count him as my best friend."

With that, I passed Sunny the present and watched him unwrap it in disbelief. After considerable protestations – he couldn't keep the watch, it wasn't his birthday, it was just too much – Sunny realised that the right thing to do was to graciously accept it.

The journey of a thousand miles begins with a single step.
Lao Tzu

MIND, SET & MATCH

I watched his face light up and realised that in buying him the watch I had actually indulged myself.

It's one of life's great paradoxes that you can't give without receiving.

You can do anything – but you can't do everything.
David Allen

Entertaining Angels

One stormy night, many years ago, an elderly man and his wife entered the lobby of a small hotel in Philadelphia, hoping to find shelter for the night.

"Could you possibly give us a room?" the husband asked the clerk the front desk. The clerk, a friendly man with a winning smile, looked at the couple and explained that there were three conventions in town.

"All of our rooms are taken," he said. "But I can't send a nice couple like you out in the rain at this time of night. Would you perhaps be willing to sleep in my room? It's not exactly a suite, but it will be good enough to make you folks comfortable for the night."

The couple declined, but the clerk insisted. "Don't worry about me, I'll make out just fine," he told them. So the couple agreed.

As he paid his bill the next morning, the elderly man said to the clerk, "You are the kind of manager who should be the boss of the best hotel in the United States. Maybe someday I'll build one for you."

The clerk looked at the couple and smiled. The three of them had a good laugh. As they drove away, the elderly couple agreed that the helpful clerk was indeed exceptional. Finding friendly people who go out of their way to be helpful isn't always easy.

Do the thing and you will have the power.
Ralph Waldo Emerson

Two years passed. The clerk had forgotten the incident when he received a letter from the old man. It recalled that stormy night and enclosed a round-trip ticket to New York, asking the young man to pay them a visit.

The old man met him in New York and led him to the corner of Fifth Avenue and 34th Street. He then pointed to a great new building there, a palace of reddish stone, with turrets and watchtowers soaring up to the sky.

"That," said the old man, "is the hotel I have just built. I want you to manage it."

"You must be joking," the young man said.

"I can assure you that I'm not," said the other, a sly smile playing around his mouth.

The old man's name was William Waldorf Astor, and the magnificent structure was the original Waldorf-Astoria Hotel. The young clerk who became its first manager was George C. Boldt.

This young clerk could never have foreseen the turn of events that would lead him to take charge of one of the world's most glamorous hotels.

You should always seek to help those who are in need. You never know, you might be welcoming an angel.

Most of the things worth doing in the world were said to be impossible before they were done.
Louis Brandeis

Pick More Daisies

When the late Nadine Stair of Louisville, Kentucky, was 85 years old, she was asked what she would do if she had to live her life over again.

"I'd make more mistakes," she said. "I'd relax. I would limber up. I would be sillier than I've been on this trip. I would take fewer things seriously. I would take more chances. I would climb more mountains and swim more rivers. I would eat more ice cream and less beans. I might have more actual troubles, but I'd have fewer imaginary ones.

"You see, I'm one of those people who live sensibly and sanely hour after hour, day after day. Oh, I've had my moments, and if I had to do it over again, I'd have more of them. In fact, I'd try to have nothing else. Just moments, one after another.

"I've been the kind of person who never goes anywhere without a thermometer, a hot water bottle and a raincoat. If I had to do it over again, I would travel lighter than I have.

" I would start barefoot earlier in the spring and stay that way later in the fall. I would go to more dances. I would ride more merry-go-rounds and pick more daisies."

Remember when you were at your best?
Now be there again.
Andrew Mead

Live your Values

It's essential to know who you really are before deciding what you really want. Many people ask themselves:

- where am I going?
- how am I going to get there?

But most importantly forget to ask:

- who am I?

When I'm coaching people on how best to manage their careers and realise their work aspirations, it never ceases to amaze me that the vast majority are looking for a job that they can fit into, rather than ask themselves "how does the job fit me?"

Your behaviour should be driven by your values, because these tell who you really are. These are the things that are most important to you. An easy way of eliciting your values is to make a list of at least twenty people who you admire, from Leonardo da Vinci to Leonardo di Caprio, and then write down the qualities that you admire in them.

You will then have a list of your values. Now prioritise these values and make a list of the top seven. These values are at the core of who you are, and violating them would be abhorrent to you. For example, included in my top seven values are 'making a difference', 'freedom' and 'creativity'. If I were in a job which was routine, with little scope for

Live out of your imagination instead of out of your memory.
Les Brown

creativity or self-expression, and which made little impact on anyone, then my spirit would start to wither.

Any behaviour which isn't consistent with your values will leave you feeling unhappy and unfulfilled. You can easily check to see if you're living your values. Score a mark out of ten for how well you're living each of your top seven. If you have a few low scores, then it's likely that you're feeling unfulfilled.

Unfortunately many organisations are intent on controlling their employees, when what their people value most is the freedom to express themselves. It's this disconnect between the values of the employer and those of the employee that leads to people jumping ship or exhibiting 'presenteeism' – they are there in body, but not in spirit. Fortunately, a growing number of organisations are trying to motivate their employees by listening to what they want to achieve and developing 'life' programmes that benefit both parties.

Ask yourself, if you were granted a wish and could achieve anything you wanted and knew that you couldn't fail, what would you do with your life? Is this what you're doing now? What would you get from your new life that you're not getting now?

Once you've determined your values you're in a position to create your vision.

There will come a time when you believe that everything is finished. That will be the beginning.

Louis L'Amour

Mind's Eye

I was a speaker at a company's end-of-year conference in the South of France recently and was asked by the CEO to talk about vision, as he felt the company could have achieved much more than it did.

Before my speech I canvassed opinion among the delegates and it quickly became clear that quite a few had not understood the company's vision, or the rationale behind it, and did not feel inspired and motivated. One manager said to me, "I don't understand why we need to spend so much time banging on about vision."

Well, a vision gives you a sense of purpose and direction. It will give you a sense of meaning and continuity to your life. Your vision gives you something to aim for and something to live for.

It provides the motivation you need to transform yourself and your life.

Without a vision we're like a ship without a rudder, drifting without purpose, tossed this way and that by events and circumstances that sometimes overwhelm us. We're not reaching for the heights, we're settling for less, and as we settle we begin to sink.

At first we may be merely bored, but if we continue to let ourselves drift, we can become depressed or even destructive to ourselves or others.

**We cannot do everything at once, but
we can do something at once.**
Calvin Coolidge

Finally, we go bitter and heavy hearted to the grave, haunted by regret, appalled by the knowledge that we missed so much.

Nothing comes into being without it first appearing as an image in someone's mind.

Your vision must be totally compelling and inspirational for you. It must set your being on fire with intensity and desire. Think big, and don't restrict yourself. What are you dreams? If you could really have the perfect life, what would this look like? How would it feel? How does this vision differ from where you are now?

It's my experience that many people have a clear idea of what they don't want, but are not so clear about what they do want. You must have a clear vision, otherwise you won't be able to channel your energies properly.

You can't take the right action unless you've got a clear picture. If your vision is hazy your action will be slow and cautious. Your vision gives you the confidence that you need for taking positive, sustained action. The clearer you are about what you're trying to create, the easier it is to make it happen.

A simple exercise to help you to create your vision is to imagine that you have lived the life of your dreams and you are now on your deathbed, surrounded by family and friends. You feel at peace with the world and ready to leave it. Now write your obituary. What was the message of your life? What do you want to be remembered for? What was your

If you don't know where you're going, any road will take you there.
Proverb

MIND, SET & MATCH

most important contribution? Why? What were your most meaningful experiences? Why?

People often lose their way in life, not because they want too much, but because they accept too little. It's amazing what a clear vision, added to desire, can achieve.

In the 1840s in a small town in Germany a young boy became fascinated with the steam engine and all things mechanical. He became convinced that, useful as steam was, there must be a better way to build an engine, and dreamed of the day when he would build the best engines in the world. On a piece of paper he drew a three-pointed star which he would put on all his engines.

The young boy's name was Gottlieb Daimler.

In 1769, a little son was born to Charles and Letizia. The boy had several brothers and sisters, and their mother, having only one servant, had little time to look after the children. So she gave them a big room to play in. The walls and floor were bare and the room was empty except for the children's toys. Here they were allowed to do as they liked. They scribbled and drew pictures on the walls and amused themselves with all sorts of games.

The young boy always drew soldiers marching to battle, and played with nothing but a drum, a wooden sword and some toy soldiers. He used to organise mock battles with the boys of the neighbourhood. The wars on the walls of the play

We work to become, not to acquire.
Elbert Hubbard

room would last for months at a time, with many fierce fights, surprises and assaults.

The boy told his mother that he wanted to be a great leader in charge of his own army when he grew up. His parents always encouraged him and told him that he could be whatever he wanted. If it was to be one of the greatest leaders in history, then so be it. With the belief and wholehearted support of his parents, the boy grew up thinking that it was perfectly natural for his dream to be fulfilled.

The boy's name was Napoleon Bonaparte.

When you have complete clarity on what you want, what purpose this serves and moreover, how this reconciles with your authentic self, then you are well on your way to achieving the results that you want.

Quality begins with character.
Amos Laurence

MIND, SET & MATCH

People vs. Things

Remember what's really important in life.

The late, great Randy Pausch told a wonderful story of how he drove his brand new VW Golf convertible to see his nephew and niece and take them out for a drive. His sister, their mother, told the children that they had to be very careful in Uncle Randy's new car. "I want your shoes to be clean when you get in the car, make sure your hands are clean, don't eat while you are in the car," and so on, and so on.

Suddenly she noticed that the children, Laura and Chris, were laughing. She couldn't understand why until she realised that Uncle Randy was pouring out a can of Coke on the front seat of his pristine new automobile.

Later that day Randy and the kids came home and the kids told their mother what a fantastic day out they had just enjoyed. Their favourite uncle clearly knew how to show them a good time. However, on the way back home, Chris had become ill and was sick on the seats.

Randy's nephew meant infinitely more to him than the car. He was very glad that Chris knew he wouldn't get into trouble for being sick on the seat, because he had seen his own uncle christen the car with Coke.

It is literally true that you can succeed best and quickest by helping others to succeed.
Napoleon Hill

Start Now

Begin doing the work you love as soon as possible, even if you don't get paid for it or can only do it part-time. Albert Einstein was unable to secure a job as a physics professor. Apparently no-one thought he was sufficiently qualified.

He could have said to himself, "Oh well, I just don't have what it takes to work in physics. I should give up and settle for something else." Instead, he wrote the two most significant papers of his remarkable career while employed as a patents clerk. After their publication there wasn't a major university in the world which would not have been delighted to have him on their staff.

The Wright brothers weren't professional scientists, but the owners of a small bicycle shop who had a passion for exploring the possibility of manned flight. Time and again, hobbies and interests outside work hold the key to an individual's true calling.

Start the business you're dreaming of out of your home or garage. Apple Computers began this way. Even if you only have evenings and weekends to work at it, make a start. There's something about just doing the work you love that attracts opportunities and opens doors.

Julie, a good friend of my wife, studied ceramics at university. It was here that she met her husband David, who was studying sculpture. After university Julie and David decided to get

Continuous effort, not strength or intelligence, is the key to unlocking our potential
Winston Churchill

MIND, SET & MATCH

office jobs in London to pay the bills while they followed their respective passions. Julie started to sell her ceramics and jewellery at a weekend market and David sold two guitars for nearly £2,000 each, with orders for several more. Neither could keep up with the demand for their work, so they decided to sell their flat and move to a much cheaper cottage in the country. This had a small outbuilding which they converted to a workshop.

Within 12 months Julie was supplying her products to Harrods and David's custom-built premium-price guitars were selling like hot cakes in the USA after one of his customers had gone back to New York and told his guitar-playing buddies.

My accountant, Peter, studied biological sciences at university and became completely enthused by plants, to the extent that he majored in botany. But when it came to leaving university and starting a career, he chose accountancy because he didn't believe that he could earn the money he wanted from gardening and landscape design.

Over time Peter became a friend and told me that he couldn't wait to retire so that he could focus on his true passion of designing and growing wonderful gardens. To Peter, the garden was the best room of his house and he would spend as much time as possible there.

Peter invited my family and me to a barbecue at his house. I had never seen his garden before, but the moment I set eyes

People wish to be settled. Only as far as they are unsettled is there any hope for them.
Ralph Waldo Emerson

SET YOURSELF ON FIRE

on it, I fell in love with it. On a glorious summer's day the kaleidoscope of colours and fantastic array of plants, shrubs and trees was truly breathtaking.

During the course of the afternoon Peter showed me the new house which he and his family were moving to the following week. It had an acre of untouched land where he could indulge his passion. He showed me his plans for the garden and it was clear that Peter was very serious about his passion, to the extent that he had become a real expert.

"When you move into your new house, let your neighbours know what you've got planned for your garden", I said to Peter. "They too will have a plot of land with maybe some grass but little else. Maybe they could use your help."

Peter took on board my advice and told his neighbours to look out for the changing landscape that was his garden. Slowly but surely they started to ask for advice and help, until one day one of them came round and said, "I want to hire you to design and plant my garden."

Peter explained that he worked full-time as an accountant, but his neighbour would have none of it. In the end they agreed to work together evenings and weekends and hire labouring help when needed. The result was a fantastic garden and a very happy customer.

So the seed was sown. Peter got more and more requests for landscape design, most of which he turned down for lack of

When you reach out, chances are pretty good that someone will reach back.
Cheryl Richardson

time. He did, however, make time to help his neighbours.

Twelve months after Peter moved in, a director from the house builders came to inspect the estate. He couldn't help but notice how wonderful most of the gardens were looking. Talking to residents on his walkabout, the director soon learned that Peter was the architect of what he saw.

The following week the Director invited Peter to meet him to discuss a business proposition. The outcome was that Peter went into partnership with the house builder and designed a range of services which would appeal to owners of new houses with a similar plot of undeveloped land.

Peter's new business was a roaring success. The jewel in the crown was the Stage Garden. This option offered a service which designed a garden in stages over one to three years. Each element would be paid for as it was completed. This allowed the new owner to have a beautiful garden within months, which would develop over the next two or three years into something quite sumptuous. This allowed owners to budget over time and didn't require payment of a lump sum up front so soon after the expense of moving home.

Peter is not only happier than he has ever been, but is also earning much more than he ever did as an accountant.

If you want to be a writer and are making your living as a waiter, don't think of yourself as a waiter who hopes one day to be a writer. That puts the work you love somewhere off

To reach any significant goal, you must leave your comfort zone.
Hyrum W. Smith

SET YOURSELF ON FIRE

in the distant future. Rather, think of yourself as a writer, temporarily supporting yourself by waiting tables – and write as much as you can.

It's possible to earn a living wage as a waiter working twenty-five hours a week at some of the better restaurants in the major cities. That leaves plenty of time to devote to training or developing your craft. Or simplify your lifestyle and reduce the number of hours you work at your current job. Even without a change in lifestyle, most people can find a few hours a week to devote to retraining, developing their craft, or working part-time in a new career – if they really want to.

What would happen if you told your employer what you really wanted to do with your life? They may be forward-looking enough to help you and create a work scenario that works better for both parties.

I once employed a young lady called Hannah. She was in her mid-twenties and had left university a couple of years earlier with a degree in French. Hannah worked as recruiter for a large multinational where I was Head of Talent & Resourcing. We were in the process of establishing our European headquarters in Paris, so her language skills would be very useful.

It was evident that Hannah was a very hard worker who was committed to delivering a great service. However, when not with a customer, Hannah was inclined to complain about the

Be the best version of yourself, not a second rate version of someone else.
Sunil Bali

MIND, SET & MATCH

work she was doing and this was having a negative effect on those around her.

So one day I asked Hannah out for lunch at a local Italian which I knew she liked. I congratulated her on the excellent work she was doing and asked how she was enjoying her job and how she saw her career progressing. She said all the things I expected, like "The job's good, I'm enjoying it and I'd like to be promoted to a managerial role within the next two years." But her responses lacked enthusiasm and conviction.

We ordered some wine and I was surprised how much Hannah knew about it. She explained that she had discovered passion for wine when she did a year's student placement in Montpellier, the capital of the Languedoc region in the south of France and the home of some very fine wines.

Then suddenly she blurted out, "I loved my time in France and would love to go and work there." She looked a little flustered so I reassured her by saying, "There's no crime in being honest. I'd like to help. What can I do to help you fulfil your dream?"

"Well, I'd like to work in a commercial role in the wine industry," she said. "To do that, I need to show that I'm serious by passing the Wine and Spirit Education Trust's Diploma. This would help me get the sort of job that I want in the industry. Then I could work towards the Master of Wine exams."

The world can only be grasped by action, not by contemplation. The hand is the cutting edge of the mind.
Jacob Bronowski

The result of our lunch was that I sponsored Hannah to study for the Diploma. It wasn't very expensive, but it did require her to attend college one afternoon per week. In return I had a very happy employee who spent the next two years delighting her customers and colleagues before leaving to work for a wine exporter.

We need to have courage and take a risk by doing work which we're passionate about and which brings us joy. This is the work that feels natural and intuitively right to us. Once we do this, everything else falls into place.

It may take courage to change job or move into a new field altogether. Will I be able to pay the mortgage? What will people say – he couldn't hack it, he couldn't handle the pressure, he's opted out? Will my parents approve? You may lose a sense of identity that's wrapped up in your job title. But you really do need to be yourself and overcome these limiting beliefs, as this is the only way that you'll achieve real happiness.

When it comes to overcoming obstacles and personal growth, the greatest breakthroughs occur when we're seemingly at the end of our talents and energy. If we persevere, stay focused on our purpose and remain detached from our results, we won't find it a struggle or become frustrated or discouraged when the going gets tough.

It takes great courage to be nobody but yourself in a world where the pressure to conform is constant and unrelenting.

I haven't failed. I've just found 10,000 ways that didn't work
Thomas Edison

It's one of the hardest challenges that we'll ever face, to be the person we really are.

In my own case, I made a list of all the head-hunters who knew me and one by one told them that I would never be on the market again because I was carving out a new career as a speaker, author and coach. Sure it was scary, but it was something I simply had to do.

Despite this, one head-hunter, a good friend of mine, persuaded me to go for an interview for a prestigious and extremely well paid job with a large multinational. I went to see the CEO and we got on exceptionally well. It soon became clear that the match was a very good one and we got to talking about life and interests outside of work.

As I started to explain why I was passionate about helping others to fulfil their potential, it dawned on me that I was far more interested in speaking, becoming an author and coaching than I was about the job on offer.

So towards the end of our discussion I just said to the CEO, "Look, whether you are going to offer me the job or not, I don't think it's right that I join you as my heart simply wouldn't be in it."

The CEO replied, "After hearing how passionate you are about what you really want to do, I agree with you. There is one thing I would like to ask you though. Can you please come and speak at our management conference later this

Carpe diem (seize the day).
Horace

year?"

And this is exactly what I did, with great success and to rave reviews.

So stop waiting until you finish school ... until you go back to school ... until you lose ten pounds ... until you gain ten pounds ... until you have kids ... until your kids leave home ... until you start work ... until you retire ... until you get married ... until you get divorced ... until Friday night ... until Sunday morning ... until you get a new car or home ... until your car or home is paid off ... until spring, until summer ... until winter ... until you are off welfare ... until the first or fifteenth ... until your song comes on ... until you've had a drink ... until you've sobered up ... until you die ... until you are born again, to decide that:

There is no better time to be happy than right now.

Work is love made visible.
Kahlil Gibran

MIND, SET & MATCH

CHAPTER 5

LIFE REWARDS ACTION

Motion Creates Emotion

How many times have you heard that knowledge is power? It seems to have become the mantra of the 21st century. There is an army of people who have paid heed to this mantra, have taken course after course, acquired real and meaningful knowledge – and then done absolutely nothing with it.

It reminds me of the advice that one of my professors gave me when I was at university: "You can only be given marks for what you put on the exam paper, not for what's in your head."

Knowledge *with action* is power.

The only place your dream won't find you is sitting around doing nothing apart from willing success to beat a path to your door. You won't find success before action, either in the dictionary or in life.

The most difficult thing to overcome is inertia. Once you're moving and have wholly committed yourself to a course of action, you'll be pleasantly surprised at how you gain momentum and how events conspire to speed you on your way. Be like a heat-seeking missile that locks onto and moves relentlessly towards its target. But be sure to launch yourself first and keep moving. Just like a missile, it's only when you're moving that you can alter course to reach your objective.

Energy is required to transform your thoughts into reality and it is forward motion toward your goal that creates positive

The distance is nothing; it is only the first step that is difficult.
Mme. Du Deffand

emotion. The greater the energy, the more likely you are to achieve your goals; the more intense the emotion, the quicker you will get there.

Keep moving forward. If you don't, you will stand still or go backwards. When you stand still you lose your momentum and have to overcome inertia all over again. This requires more effort than maintaining speed, just as a car uses more fuel on stop-start journeys than cruising down the highway.

The biggest fear that most people face when doing work for enjoyment's sake is how they will make enough money. Once they take persistent action in the direction of their dreams, this hurdle is overcome.

Keep doing what you do with a smile on your face and the universe will take care of the rest. Start to live the life of your dreams one step at a time and before you know it, you'll actually be living the life of your dreams.

If I look at my career to date and how I've been successful, I've always done what I could from where I was. I soon realised that everything that occurred in my past, whether good or bad, had value because I had learned what I needed to and kept moving forward.

Whenever I've fallen flat on my face – and it's happened a few times – I've picked myself up and found that despite the failure I was still further forward than if I'd done nothing at all.

The great danger is not that our aim is too high and we miss it, but that it is too low and we reach it.
Michelangelo

It's amazing how the people and resources that I've needed to carry on my journey have miraculously appeared when I've needed them. It's a common trait of happy people that they stay positive and focused on doing what they can, and leave the rest to the universe.

What is the smallest thing you can do right now, that could give the biggest change moving forward? Just do it, no matter how tiny it is.

You'll find that each positive step you take, no matter how small or seemingly insignificant, will stimulate another positive step. It's called the snowball effect and it has the power to alter your life forever.

You don't need to give up your job. If you want to write, write an outline of what you want to be published. If you want to start a business, then start researching it and talk to people in the know. There is always something you can do to move in the direction of your dreams, so don't wait. Take action now.

I was born in Kenya, the homeland of the Masai tribe. They have a saying which roughly translates as:

"Whether you're a lion or a gazelle, when you wake in the morning be ready to shift your backside and run. If you don't, you'll either go hungry or die."

> **Education is not filling a bucket but lighting a fire.**
> W.B. Yeats

Amateur vs. Professional

My friend and author of the best selling book *The Work We Were Born To Do*, Nick Williams, likens the process of success to being a professional. If you're serious about being successful then you'll have a disciplined and professional approach to everything you do. This includes managing your time effectively. If you think like an amateur, waiting for inspiration to strike, then your chances of success are severely diminished.

As the author of five wonderful books, Nick knows the importance of ensuring that he writes consistently every week.

Somerset Maugham once said, "I write only when inspiration strikes. Fortunately, it strikes promptly at 9 o'clock every morning."

Research has shown that there is a direct correlation between self-discipline and self-esteem. Those individuals who have high levels of self awareness, who have control of their minds and therefore their lives, have much higher levels of self-esteem and confidence. These people, when you meet them, come across as well balanced and centred. They radiate happiness.

The more you do the things that you know you should, the more pleased you'll be with yourself. The more confidence you have, the more likely you are to overcome obstacles. Self-

Formal education will make you a living, but self-education will make you a fortune.
Jim Rohn

discipline increases your self-confidence, and vice versa - the two feed off each other.

The more action you take and the more connections you make, the more chances you give the universe to act on your behalf. Synchronicity, serendipity and coincidence: all these things can occur frequently in your life, but only if you keep taking action.

As the ice hockey great Wayne Gretzky said, "You miss 100% of the shots that you don't take."

Don't concern yourself with how far you are from realising your desires. Instead, engage in the creative process and trust that in time it will deliver your vision. Commit yourself 100% to the process of creating the life that you want and simply let it unfold. If you think the cost of success is high, the cost of failure is higher.

Only those who will risk going too far can possibly find out how far one can go.
T.S. Eliot

Congruent Triangles

If you cast your mind back to your geometry lessons at school, you may remember coming across congruent triangles. These are triangles that have the same size and shape. Two triangles are congruent if their sides are the same length and their internal angles correspond exactly. When superimposed, they coincide exactly at every point.

To be successful your unconscious mind must be congruent with your conscious mind. If they do not match it's extremely difficult to be successful. This lack of congruence between conscious and unconscious is the primary reason why people don't live the life that they want.

Let's suppose that you want to earn over £250k a year. You think about this in your conscious mind, but subconsciously you don't actually believe that this will happen. Guess what will happen? You can use as much conscious willpower as you want, but it won't be enough if deep down you don't have the confidence and belief.

If, however, your goals are an expression of your true self, then your belief and desire will act as a catalyst and propel you forward.

You'll know that you're thinking congruently when meaningful events - what Jung termed synchronicity - occur more and more frequently. This is what happens when your subconscious mind connects with the universe. For example,

Those who reach greatness on earth reach it through concentration.
Upanishads

I saw an article on some of the issues facing a public sector organisation and I thought to myself that, given my experience and skills, I could really help them. I also thought that working with them would give me an opportunity to put something back into my local community.

I became quite excited at the prospect and decided that I must make contact and explore how I could help. Later that day, quite by chance, I met someone from the organisation. Within a few weeks I had joined the board as a non-executive director.

Assuming your goals are congruent, you'll be amazed how many targets on your list you'll have achieved at the end of twelve months. Moreover, you'll be astounded at the very considerable synchronicity that has occurred over the year.

The reason this works is that the act of writing out congruent goals is like planting seeds in your subconscious. If you water these seeds daily with belief and expectation, they will grow, mature and bear fruit when the time is right. The ultimate goal is to master yourself and be happy. The journey to mastery is life.

It's as if taking action puts you on a track where you attract all the knowledge, resources and people that you need. There may be stops along the way, but all you need to do is keep taking focused action in the direction of your dreams and listen to your heart. By taking consistent action, and taking

> **You can't build a reputation on what you're going to do. It's simple, fantasise, rehearse, then go out into the world and do it.**
> Henry Ford

responsibility for where we are at any given point, we keep our creative energy flowing.

Set big goals. Don't be constrained or small-minded. Set goals with a wow factor – goals which when you achieve them, will make your heart sing. Let the goal inspire you. The inspiration will put a smile to your face.

Discipline is the bridge between goals and accomplishment.
Jim Rohn

The Top 5%

At Schipol Airport, Amsterdam, the toilets are kept scrupulously clean. So it is surprising to find an insect in the bowl of the men's urinal. Even more surprising is the fact that every bowl has a fly in it. Closer inspection reveals that the 'fly' is a picture that has been etched into the porcelain.

Why? It improves the aim. If a man sees a fly he aims at it. Insect-in-urinal research has found that fly etchings reduce spillage by over 80%. It gives a guy something to think about.

The same is true of goals. If you set yourself goals you dissipate far less energy, since you've got something to aim for.

Most people don't have any clear goals or vision and are then surprised that they don't get what they want. But how can you hit a target that you can't see? More than 95% of adults don't have any written goals. The simple act of writing out your goals will put you in the top 5% of the population.

The number one fear for most people is the fear of rejection. Why is this? It's because we measure of our efforts in terms of whether the world accepts us or rejects us. This is the reason why many people don't set goals. If you don't have a goal, you can't fail.

Success is not an accident. Research clearly shows that successful people plan for and expect success. They have clear

**Start by doing what you can, then by doing what is possible;
before you know it you are doing the impossible.**

St. Francis of Assisi

goals and are totally focussed and committed. Non-achievers either have no goals, or have goals which aren't congruent. Typically, they are trying to achieve something that someone else wants, or seeking another's approval.

If you don't create a plan for your own life, the chances are that you'll fall into someone else's plan. And guess what they have planned for you? Not as much as you want. Other people may be happy to place their future in someone else's hands. Don't let it be you.

The most difficult problem can be solved if it is broken down into smaller chunks – after all, you can only take one step at a time. Break down your big life goals into bite-size tasks. Big problems don't seem so daunting once they're broken down, and as you deal with each chunk your confidence will grow. As your confidence grows, the bigger the chunks you can tackle. Write down what you want in detail so that it becomes clear in your mind. For anything to happen in the real world, it must first be created in the imagination.

Prioritise your goals and decide which one will have the most positive effect on your life. This primary goal will be congruent with your purpose in life. Focusing on your primary goal will make for better decisions and choices.

To do this, write out your goals as a personal statement. Write it in the present tense. For example, if you wish to earn £100k a year write: "I earn £100k per year." If your goal is to write a best-selling book, write: "My book is a bestseller."

We gain strength by sharing strength.
Don Ward

LIFE REWARDS ACTION

Carry these cards with you and read them every morning and every night before you go to bed, or before you meditate, so that they are firmly installed in your subconscious.

When you read your affirmations do so with intense emotion - the emotion that you'll have when you do earn £100k per year or when you see your book on the bestsellers shelf.

Visualise these events as if they're happening now. Experience the emotion: it could be joy, freedom, a sense of achievement. Go one step further: visualise what you're doing with your new-found wealth. The greater your emotion, the quicker the subconscious mind will influence the universe to make your thoughts a reality. Repeat this visualisation process every day, in the same way that an athlete visualises winning a race. You can use this process to achieve whatever you want in your life whether it's a new career, a new relationship, more wealth – anything.

Now consider what actions you can take quickly to meet your goals, particularly your primary goal. Again, write down your action plan. Developing an action plan will give you greater clarity and confidence. It will also make you more aware of the opportunities, people and resources that can help you.

Assign timescales and deadlines. Write down how you'll measure your progress, and how you'll know that you have achieved your goals. This is very important. When you can show yourself that you're making progress towards your goals, you stay motivated.

There is no security in life, only opportunity.
Mark Twain

Analysis Paralysis

When all's said and done, a lot more is said than done.

Don't wait to be perfect before setting out on the path to your dreams. You don't have to be the world expert in your field. Too many people suffer analysis paralysis and never get round to taking that first all-important step. I call it death by procrastination.

This doesn't mean that you don't set yourself the highest standards, but rather that you won't let your lack of perfection stop you from taking action.

Many people don't take action because their proposition is not 100% right. It's OK to settle for less than perfect. All of us are learning. Besides, does anyone ever reach perfection?

Nothing would be done at all if a man waited until he could do it so well that no one could find fault with it.

Cardinal Newman

Questions Are the Answer

As a psychotherapist, perhaps the single most powerful technique that I have come across is reframing. Reframing helps you to see the positive in the negative, and the good motive in the bad behaviour. One of the most effective ways of reframing is to ask the right question.

During my clinical training I regularly encountered statements such as "I never feel happy" and "Bad things always happen to me." My response is to reframe these statements by asking questions such as "Can you remember a time that you felt happy?" or "So you've never ever smiled?" or "Starting from the day you were born, give me one example of when you were happy and smiled."

By asking empowering questions of ourselves and others we change the quality of our lives. Questions enable you to change or keep your focus where it is needed, to achieve the results that you want.

For example, if you see a wonderful property which looks like your dream house, rather than say to yourself, "I'll never be able to afford that," ask yourself: "What do I need to do to be able to afford a house like that?"

Virtually all the people I have coached to lose weight have told me, "I can't lose weight." I reframe their response as a question: "So you haven't found a way yet to maintain your ideal weight?"

People are not lazy. They simply have impotent goals.
Anthony Robbins

Overweight people continually ask themselves disempowering questions. "What food can't I eat?" "What can I get away with eating, which will fill me up?" Reframed, the questions become empowering: "Will eating this food help me to look and feel great?" "What nutritious and tasty food can I eat that will leave me feeling good because I'm still on target to reach my ideal weight?"

When I start coaching people, in the first session I ask them: "What action have you taken to get to where you are today?" Then I ask: "What do you think you need to do differently to achieve the success that you want?" I do this to check if they have asked themselves the right questions, because it's not only the questions that you ask, but also the ones you don't ask, which shape your destiny.

Successful people ask great questions of themselves and others. As a result they get great answers.

Even when faced with failure and rejection, winners ask themselves: "What can I learn from this situation so that I get it right next time?"

If you don't know the answer to your question you can bet that someone else does.

There is no such thing as failure, only feedback.
Thomas Edison

Dream Support

Whatever you want to do in your life, there's a very good chance that someone else has done it already and left a trail of knowledge which you can tap into. This knowledge might be in a book, a newspaper or magazine interview, on the internet, at a seminar or lecture. All you have to do is find it. Ideally, talk to people who are successful and find out how they achieved it. It's amazing how helpful people can be if you tell them that you admire their work and wish to learn from them.

Model yourself on these people and try to identify the factors behind their success. These will undoubtedly include the quality of their thinking, since successful people think successful thoughts. Learn from others who have achieved great things and immerse yourself in success stories and the literature of positive psychology. By doing so you'll be inspired to achieve your dreams and realise that you really can think your way to success.

Napoleon Hill employed a useful technique which he called the Mastermind Principle. This involves creating a kind of peer group of the mind. By reading the life stories and the writings of the greats of history, you begin to identify with them as people like yourself. You break down the barrier between yourself and greatness. As you make friends with great people you begin to engage them in mental conversation, seeking insight, advice and direction. You start to think the

To know oneself, one should assert oneself.
Albert Camus

MIND, SET & MATCH

kind of thoughts they think and raise your expectations of yourself.

Whatever your chosen field, identify the leaders and find out what made them successful. Many successful people have simply modelled themselves on those people they aspire to be. Don't waste time reinventing the wheel; learn from the experts in your field. My mastermind group includes one of the world's best speakers, a best-selling author and a leading adviser to the UK government. I outsource those areas where I have little expertise, and acquiring it would distract me from my core focus. This includes working with specialists in public relations and social media.

While creating a mastermind group is very powerful, just as important is the company we keep in daily life. Spend your time with people who energise you and dispense with, or at least minimise, the time you spend with those people who are toxic and drain you of energy.

People can't believe in you any more than they can believe in themselves. The only people who can consistently wish you happiness are those who are themselves consistently happy. The only ones who can inspire you to excellence are those who are committed to it.

Think about and list the names of people you would like to get to know better; people who could serve as role models or supportive friends.

Failure is simply a few errors in judgement, repeated every day.
Jim Rohn

Networking = Not Working

Don't hide your light. All things being equal, it's people who are the most visible who will be successful. Don't be the best-kept secret in town. Keep putting yourself out there. It's only when you transmit that you can engage. If you're not out there, the opportunities can't find you.

Networking and connecting with others is hugely rewarding, and is the quickest way to find the people, resources and opportunities that you want. Nevertheless, many people snatch defeat from victory simply because they don't seek the support they need to reach the winning line. Isolation is a dream killer.

Take a genuine interest in others and they will reciprocate. Put yourself in other people's shoes and try to see the world through their eyes. By doing this you'll find it easier to understand other people's perspective and will build rapport quickly and effortlessly.

Listen to others first to find out how you can help them. If you can't, then don't be afraid to ask "How can I help you?" Remember, what goes around, comes around. They will then listen to you and want to help you.

By giving freely of yourself, you'll increase your power of attraction. You'll act like a magnet, drawing towards you people and resources to speed you towards your goals.

Leaders have no interest in proving themselves, but an abiding interest in expressing themselves.
Warren Bennis

I keep a dream book which contains some of my achievements to date and pictures of what I want to achieve in the future. I've acquired this tool from other successful people that I know. If I'm feeling a little low on confidence – it happens occasionally! – my dream book reminds me what I'm capable of.

My dream book also helps me to celebrate the synchronicity and the benevolence of the universe which have helped me to achieve success.

The reason dream books are useful is because the pictures take you straight to where you want to be. You bypass the "how" – the process of getting there – and focus on your goal.

Another technique which I find very useful to change my state of mind, if I'm not feeling particularly positive or energised, is "breaking state."

Some things that help me to break out of a negative state include playing electric guitar, reading inspirational literature, exercise and playing sport, playing with my kids, listening to music – I have compiled two CDs of my favourite music which I've entitled Statebreakers – and looking at my dream book.

He who can copy can do.
Leonardo da Vinci

Me Ltd.

Build your personal brand and develop a reputation for being among the very best at what you do.

The best way to achieve any degree of job security is to continually invest in self improvement and use your knowledge proactively.

Excellence, like mediocrity, is a habit. Quality breeds quality. Do one thing well, and you'll want the rest to come up to the same standard. Make a habit of cutting corners and you end up wondering whether you're ever capable of quality work. This is one reason why it's vital to do your best, even if the work that you're currently doing doesn't seem important or meaningful. Once made, habits are difficult to break.

People who are committed to excellence don't rest on their laurels; neither do they dwell on their mistakes. The expectation of success allows them to put their mistakes and failings in the proper context. Of course, commitment to excellence requires a willingness to accept feedback, to examine and address our shortcomings, whether in character or competence. But those who succeed are those who quickly assimilate what they need to learn and bounce back.

Don't complain. Complaining is a complete waste of energy.

Prepare for success by continually seeking to improve the skills that will enable you to achieve your goals. If you lack

Difficulties make you a jewel.
Japanese proverb

a skill that you need to achieve your goal, then acquire it, delegate it or outsource it.

Be patient with yourself as certain skills take longer to acquire than others. Rome wasn't built in a day.

Leaders are readers. It's well known that people who are well educated - not necessarily academically - and who read assiduously, earn far more on average than those who don't.

Broaden your knowledge, but don't seek to acquire knowledge unless it supports your goals, or you find the acquisition of knowledge intrinsically rewarding. Remember, continuous improvement is about improving quality, not increasing quantity.

"I don't have enough time" is a phrase that I often hear. You have plenty of time to be, do or have anything you want in your life.

Re-examine your priorities, see where you're spending your time and change your focus. This will give you all the time that you need.

**You have to do it by yourself, and
you can't do it alone.**
Martin Rutte

LIFE REWARDS ACTION

Turning Lemons into Lemonade

Research has shown that one of the main reasons why people fail is not a lack of resources, ability or opportunity, but because they give up in the face of difficulties. Your persistence and determination are the true measure of your ability to succeed.

One of the greatest examples of persistence is Abraham Lincoln. Born in poverty, Lincoln encountered defeat throughout his life. He lost eight elections, twice failed in business and suffered a nervous breakdown. But he never gave up. Here is a sketch of his road to the White House:

1816   Family forced out of their home. He had to work to support them.

1818   Mother died.

1831   Failed in business.

1832   Ran for state legislature – lost. Also lost his job. Failed to get into law school.

1833   Borrowed from a friend to begin a business. Bankrupt by the end of the year. Spent the next 17 years paying off the debt.

1834   Ran for state legislature again – won.

1835   Engaged to be married. Sweetheart died.

1836   Total nervous breakdown. In bed for six months.

Great things are done by a series of small things brought together.
Vincent Van Gogh

MIND, SET & MATCH

1838 Sought to become speaker of the state legislature – defeated.

1840 Sought to become elector – defeated.

1843 Ran for Congress – lost.

1846 Ran for Congress again – won. Went to Washington and did a good job.

1848 Ran for re-election to Congress – lost.

1849 Sought job of Land Officer in his home state – rejected.

1854 Ran for US Senate – lost.

1856 Sought Vice-Presidential nomination at his party's national convention. Won less than 100 votes.

1858 Ran for US Senate again – lost.

1860 Elected President of the United States.

He could have quit many times, but he didn't. And because he didn't quit, Lincoln became one of the greatest presidents in the history of the USA.

I've been responsible for helping to manage the careers of thousands of people down the years for some of the world's biggest and most successful companies. It's never ceased to amaze me the number of talented, bright, intelligent people who are on the right path towards a successful career but snatch defeat from the jaws of victory through self-sabotage,

Sticking to it is the genius.
Thomas Edison

losing belief and losing conviction in what they're doing. They stop taking the right action and their train, although on the right tracks and heading for the right destination, just grinds to a halt.

If you set yourself congruent goals and don't give up, you'll achieve them. If you're doing what you love, it won't feel as if you've got the weight of the world on your shoulders. Quite the opposite in fact, you'll feel as if you've got the weight of the world behind you to break through any obstacles and overcome any challenges along the way.

The strongest trees are those that as saplings have been subjected to strong winds and have had to be flexible to survive. The more flexible you are, the more you'll consider different options and so have more choices to achieve your desired outcome. Whatever your plan for your life, it's almost certain that events will require you to amend your plan. But since life is in the journey, not the destination, these events represent huge opportunities for personal growth and development. Taken together, it's the sequence of events and the happiness in each moment which actually forms your life.

Thomas Edison, one of the world's great inventors, had a wonderful approach to failure. He believed that each failure was part of a process of elimination, so each setback took him one step closer to the solution. With this frame of mind, success was only a matter of time – even if it did take him over 700 attempts to come up with the incandescent light

People can't answer a call that isn't made.
Robert Morgan

bulb. As Phil Knight, the founder of Nike, said, "You only have to succeed the last time."

Edison worked from a workshop within a large warehouse. One day a neighbour alerted him that the warehouse containing his life's work was burning down. He ran to the warehouse, then ran back to fetch his wife. As they arrived at the burning building he said to her, "Isn't that the most amazing fire that you've ever seen?" That's one heck of a reframe.

History is full of examples of successful people who could also have been classified as the greatest failures for the number of times that they have failed.

The following statement was made by one of the world's greatest athletes and arguably the greatest basketball player of all time:

> "I've missed more than 9,000 shots in my career. I've lost almost 300 games. 26 times, I've been trusted to take the game winning shot and missed. I've failed over and over in my life. And that is why I succeed."
> *Michael Jordan*

Ultimate victory cannot be denied to anyone who refuses to give up. Learn to let rejection and disappointment roll off your back. Just keep moving forward. Often, the person who succeeds is the last one still willing to try after everyone else has given up.

Learning is not compulsory, but neither is survival.
W. Edwards Deming

Stay focused and concentrate on your goals. Remember what your priorities are and commit to them wholeheartedly. Look at them every day. Don't be distracted and water down your efforts. The strongest acids can burn through thick steel, but when diluted they are rendered ineffective.

A 250W light bulb will light a room very well, but if you channel 250W of light into a laser beam it will cut through metal. The power of staying focused is immense.

In my own life, whenever I've been successful it has been because I've taken consistent, focused action regardless of the circumstances: I've simply done whatever I can, with whatever I've got.

As the American Zig Ziglar said, "Life does throw up some lemons along the way in the shape of different experiences. But the great art of living is turning those lemons into lemonade."

Conform and be dull.
James Dobie

86,400 Seconds

Successful people live life to the maximum and maintain high levels of energy. They find time to work and play hard while achieving an excellent work life balance. They achieve this by not wasting their time.

Successful people maintain a keen level of awareness of what they're doing at any given point, and how this is going to benefit them. Such a person may spend an hour or two watching a film or game of football, but realises that relaxation is necessary to recharge the batteries.

However, they will not spend a whole day in front of the television working their way through a mountain of fast food. This is not only a waste of time but it also drains you of energy. If they do get around to doing something constructive, they have insufficient energy to complete it.

Make the best use of your time. Spend as much time as possible on activities which will help you achieve the results you desire.

Are you spending time on what you really want to do? If you're doing stuff that you don't want to do, there must be a way round. Perhaps you can get someone else to help. It's never too early to delegate.

You're given 86,400 seconds a day, and once they're gone you won't get them back.

It only takes one person to change your life – you.
Ruth Casey

The Mexican Fisherman

Be completely clear about what you want - and what you'll get from having it. Ask yourself, "What purpose does this goal serve?" This acts as a reality check. Is it for the greater good, or just your ego speaking? There's nothing wrong in wanting an expensive sports car if you have a passion for cars. But if you want just to show people that you can afford an expensive sports car, then this is not wise.

An American businessman was standing at the pier of a Mexican fishing village when a small boat docked. Inside the boat were one fisherman and several large yellow fin tuna. The American complimented the Mexican on the quality of his catch.

"How long did it take you to catch them?" the American asked.

"Only a little while," the Mexican replied.

"Why don't you stay out longer and catch more fish?" said the American.

"I have enough to support my family's immediate needs," the Mexican replied.

"But," the American then asked, "what do you do with the rest of your time?"

The fisherman said, "I sleep late, fish a little, play with my children, take a siesta with my wife, stroll into the village each

A dream is a wish your heart makes.
Annette Funicello

evening where I sip wine and play guitar with my amigos. I have a full and busy life, señor."

The American scoffed, "I am a Harvard MBA and I could help you. You should spend more time fishing and with the proceeds you should buy a bigger boat. With the proceeds from the bigger boat you could buy several boats. Eventually you would have a fleet of fishing boats.

"After that you could open your own canning factory. Then you could control the product, the processing and the distribution. You could leave this little village and move to Mexico City, then Los Angeles and eventually New York, where you will run your expanding enterprise."

"How long will this all take, señor?" the fisherman asked.

The American replied, "Fifteen or twenty years."

"But what then, señor?"

The American laughed. "That's the best part. When the time is right you would announce a stock market flotation and sell shares in your company and become very rich. You would make millions."

"Millions, señor? Then what?"

"Then you would retire. You could move to a small fishing village where you would sleep late, fish a little, play with your kids, take a siesta with your wife, stroll to the village in the evenings, sip wine and play your guitar with your amigos..."

Happiness is a perfume that you cannot pour on others without getting a few drops on yourself.
Ralph Waldo Emerson

CHAPTER 6

RESONATE

Resonate: *verb* –

- To evoke a feeling of shared emotion or belief.
- To correspond harmoniously.
- To exhibit resonance.

Your Innate Guidance System

Everyone has access to the voice of inspiration. It's what the Quakers call the still, small voice within. When you listen to your inner voice it lays down a path like a blueprint. This blueprint contains everything you need to know to create a wonderful life. However, that inner voice is repeatedly ignored by most people because it requires courage. It prompts you to step out of your comfort zone and defy the conventions of society. It may even prompt you to follow a path that fills your nearest and dearest with fear.

It usually starts with an inkling, a sense that there must be something more to life than a safe routine, doing the same things day after day, things which don't make you happy.

Daydreams and impulses will keep coming up, no matter how often you push them away. Every time you do this you are denying yourself your natural right to be happy by living out your inner vision.

The fact is, you already know what you want to do. The more honest you are with yourself about it, the more your own unique blueprint for a wonderful life will begin to emerge.

The only real valuable thing is intuition.
Albert Einstein

The voice of inspiration begins to speak louder and more clearly and your life will change. All you have to do is listen to your inner voice, then take the action that feels right. As the proverb says, "there are none so blind as those who will not see."

People sometimes ask me, "How do I know when I'm listening to my innate guidance system?" You know when you don't feel any fear. You feel guided and in tune with the universe. You'll be doing what you love and want to do. You'll notice that synchronicities, serendipity and apparent coincidences abound. Events unfold as if by design.

The vast majority of people practise top-down thinking; in other words they predominantly use their head to make decisions. A small number will listen to their heart and a smaller minority will also trust their gut instinct.

The fact is you need to practise bottom-up thinking. First you need to trust your gut instinct; once you've done that, listen to your heart; lastly use your head. If you tell yourself that you have to completely understand everything before you take action, then you'll severely diminish your creativity and will miss out on a great many opportunities.

By following your heart and your intuition you're far more likely to dream bigger dreams and set bigger goals, because your rational mind will be less involved in your decision making.

We are not human beings having a spiritual experience, we are spiritual beings having a human experience.
Teilhard de Chardin

I urge you strongly to listen to your IGS, because it will guide you in the direction of your dreams and help to make them come true.

Tune in to your IGS each day by being still or meditating. Effortless success will begin to follow.

A useful exercise at the end of each day is to review what actions you took during that day. Ask yourself why you did them. Was it because you had to, because you ought to, or because you actually wanted to? The more you work from desire and inspiration, the more successful and happier you'll be.

If you look at a modern day aircraft, it's actually on autopilot for most of the journey, but the pilot still has to start the engines, close the doors and get on the runway. Your autopilot is your IGS. Use your IGS to guide you to take the right action. This will be the action that feels right and which focuses you on the present moment. Staying focussed in the present moment will enable you to create your future. You don't have to fly your plane around the world, but you do have to leave the terminal and get airborne for the universe to work its magic and help you to get to your destination as easily as possible. If you want to cross the winning line you have to get out of the starting blocks.

Your job is to do the simple things and then get out of your own way.

The more I study physics, the more I am drawn to metaphysics.
Albert Einstein

MIND, SET & MATCH

Learning to trust your IGS is a skill which comes with practice. You'll master it more quickly if you pay attention to what happens when you do - or don't - listen to it. In time, you'll discover that when you follow through on what your IGS is telling you, things work out well, and when you ignore it you are heading for trouble. Trust your hunches and follow your IGS in little things and you'll be more willing to trust it with the big decisions of your life. You shouldn't rely on logic alone to decide the important things, like whom to marry or which career to pursue. Ultimately, you have to go with what your IGS is telling you.

Your IGS can give you inspirations or solutions that you would never find through other means. It can save you months, even years, of struggle by steering you away from dead ends and traps. Your IGS is there to guide you every step of the way. So pay attention to what it is telling you!

When you come to a crossroads, follow the voice of your IGS. It's the universe's role to give you hunches, it is your role to be awake to them, and not waste them. Let the universe take the burden.

We don't know who we are, until we can see what we do.
Martha Grimes

Flow

The seed of mystery lies in muddy water;
How can I perceive this mystery?
Water becomes clear through stillness;
How can I become still?
By flowing with the stream.

Lao-Tzu

Our natural state as humans is to be happy. Energy flows from and through everything and everyone around us to make that possible. When we're not getting what we want it's because we're not in tune with the world around us.

Relax and tune yourself in. Thoughts and emotions are like radio waves – you can't see them but it's as if they fill the air around you. All you need is a receiver and the ability to select the right frequency. Your mind is the receiver. The process of tuning needs a relaxed, receptive, open frame of mind. Don't try too hard; struggling and straining will impede your natural ability to receive.

Wolfgang Amadeus Mozart is said to have written down many of his finest works as if he were taking dictation. Describing his state of mind while composing, Mozart said, "It is when I am, as it were, completely myself, entirely alone, and of good cheer, that ideas flow best and most abundantly. Whence they come, I know not, nor can I force them."

A man with outward courage dares to die.
A man with inward courage dares to live.
Lao-Tzu

MIND, SET & MATCH

Have complete, unwavering faith that the universe will deliver. In this state of heightened awareness and expectation, watch out for the opportunities and situations that will undoubtedly appear.

Your feelings will guide you and let you know when you're on the right track. It may be days, weeks or even months before the universe fulfils your desire, depending on how far away it is from your present situation.

If your emotions are good and you're feeling happy, then you're on the right path: you are tuned to the right frequency and allowing the universe to speak to you.

If you're experiencing negative emotions – fear, anger, sadness or guilt – then you're misaligned. You need to get out of your own way by changing your thinking. Let your emotions act as a signal from your Innate Guidance System. As soon as you experience a negative emotion, deal with it. Replace it with a positive.

Remember, the process of asking and receiving is value neutral and will deliver against your dominant thoughts. So if your primary thoughts are negative ones then don't be surprised if you start to manifest that which you least want.

Nature supports and sustains life if it's allowed to. It will support you too if you can get out of our your own way and allow it to.

Learn to get out of your own way. Let the universe support

Without love the acquisition of knowledge only increases confusion and leads to self-destruction.
Krishnamurti

you just as its supports everything around you. You'll know when you're resisting the universe when you gauge how you're feeling. If you have low energy levels and are feeling low, or are unhappy in any way, then you're resisting the universe. So be aware of your emotions and use them to guide the quality of your thinking and direct your thoughts to support the fulfilment of your desire.

Don't resist the natural flow of well-being which is your birthright.

Even if something bad happens or a problem arises, then be aware that this is an opportunity to grow and practise being in flow with the universe.

The more time that you spend flowing with the universe, the more natural this state becomes.

You'll encounter greater synchronicity and seem to become more lucky as circumstances conspire to help you. Resources and people to help you will appear just when you need them, as if by magic.

In this kind of consciousness, life becomes a continuous stream of magical events and seeming coincidences.

The heart has its reasons that the mind knows nothing of.
Blaise Pascal

Now and Zen

There was once a seeker of enlightenment who was desperate to reach his goal. He travelled far to find a Zen master who had a reputation for guiding people quickly to their highest potential.

After a long journey the seeker arrived at the monastery. After three days of waiting, he was finally granted an audience with the master. He explained the intensity of his desire and asked how long it would take him to succeed. The master looked deeply into the seeker's eyes and said, "Twenty years." The seeker was horrified.

"What if I really apply myself? I will readily work twice as hard as any student in your monastery."

The Zen master looked amused. "Ah! Forgive me – I didn't realise the ferocity of your commitment. It will take you at least thirty years to succeed."

The seeker was confused. "You don't understand, oh Great One," he cried, "I am willing to push myself to the limits, to go the extra mile, to give one hundred and ten percent in order to achieve my goal: I crave enlightenment!"

"I see" replied the master, "In that case it will take no less than forty years to find what you are seeking."

He who knows others is wise, he who knows himself is enlightened.
Lao-Tzu

The Art of the Possible

Several years ago I was negotiating a multi-million pound management buy-out (MBO). The deal was about to collapse – a decision had been made not to proceed, and I was told that nothing could be done to change it.

This deal represented ten years of my working life. I and my team had worked hard and long to build up the business, and now I was being told it would shut down in a matter of days and we would be out of work.

I managed to maintain enough faith in myself and the universe that a solution would emerge if I fulfilled my part of the bargain and remained detached from the outcome. The reason I was able to maintain this frame of mind was that it had already seen me through a difficult divorce and a redundancy.

I trusted and believed that something would happen to save the deal. Despite my predicament I kept a smile on my face, I thought and acted positively and left the rest to the universe.

Before the aborted buy-out talks, one possibility I had considered was selling the business to a third party. But I didn't know of anyone suitable. Now, with the business on the brink, I attended a lunch and quite unexpectedly I was introduced to a CEO of a large recruitment company.

We got talking and it transpired that he was looking to sell

You must be that change which you wish to see in the world.
Mahatma Gandhi

MIND, SET & MATCH

his own business. He told me that if my business was part of the package, it would increase both the likelihood of a sale and the sale price. After three weeks of long and sometimes difficult negotiations, the deal was completed.

At the time, most impartial observers would have considered it inconceivable that an MBO would take place. But with a large dose of self-belief and trust, my team and I not only avoided the prospect of unemployment but went on to make substantial earnings over the course of the next three years.

The disciplined man masters thoughts by stillness and emotions by calmness.
Lao-Tzu

Control Your Energy, Control Your Life

Energy, not time, is the currency of high performance. The number of hours in the day is fixed, but the energy available to us isn't. It is our most precious resource.

The more we take responsibility for the energy we bring to the world, the more empowered and productive we become. The more we blame others or external circumstances, the more negative and compromised our energy is likely to be.

If you can align your working life with your deepest desires and talents, you won't have to worry about motivation. Energy will flow.

Spiritual energy, or purpose, enables you to manage your time better because you know your priorities. There's no need to try to please others because you live from a basis of internal truth.

Your energy increases when you find your purpose and have a clarity of vision, supported by well thought-out goals. People who are very clear about who they are and their mission in life tend to be full of energy.

Think about where your energy goes. How do you spend your currency? What people or activities make you feel energised and enthusiastic? Which ones drain you of energy?

Identify the energy drains in your life. Toxic relationships, unfinished business, worrying about the future, holding onto sadness or anger from past events, complaining, negative

**If our true nature is permitted to guide our life,
we grow healthy, fruitful, and happy.**
Abraham Maslow

MIND, SET & MATCH

self-talk – all these things rob you of energy that you need to realise your dreams. Deal with the things that drag you down.

Too often we waste valuable energy trying to protect our ego. As a result we have less energy available for the things that matter. Don't obsess over what other people think about you. It's a complete waste of energy. Even saints have their detractors.

Our point of reference should be ourself, and not others.

Life is about having fun and growing. To live life fully we need to become detached from people, events and material possessions. Only when we are free of these dependencies can we focus on what we were born to do. This freedom manifests in a lightness of being, a sense of joy, creativity and a zest for life.

Eliminating, or at least significantly reducing, these energy drains is the beginning of living a successful life. You may well be driving down the highway of life in a Ferrari; if your fuel tank leaks you are going nowhere fast.

Energy + Action = Manifestation

The more energised you are, the quicker your life will change for the better. Shift your focus to activities that increase your energy - read something inspirational, take some exercise, listen to interesting people - and cease the ones that drag you down. Make time to do the things you enjoy.

Your body is smarter than you think: trust it to achieve the goals you have set. The secret to winning any game is in not trying too hard.
Timothy Gallwey

As you increase your energy you'll find that it's like increasing the current through an electromagnet. You'll become a more powerful magnet, attracting more and more people who are inspired by your positive energy and enthusiasm. This in turn will create more resources and opportunities that will help you to achieve your goals.

You focus your energy with your thoughts. Learn to master your thoughts and only dwell on those that connect to your dream.

Just as a sculptor learns to mould clay to bring into form his sculpture, so you too can learn to focus your energy and channel it to sculpt your future.

If you're feeling full of energy and are happy, then there's every reason to believe that you're in tune with the universe and consequently you're allowing the universe to help you deliver your desires.

Man is a thinking reed but his great works are done when he is not calculating and thinking.
D.T. Suzuki

Human Being vs. Human Doing

To see a world in a grain of sand
And Heaven in a wild flower
Hold infinity in the palm of your hand
And Eternity in an hour
William Brake

A key component of life mastery is achieving more by doing less.

To do this, it's essential to spend some time each day as a human being rather than a human doing. It is by intermittently disengaging that we are able to passionately re-engage with life. The French have an expression, *reculer pour mieux sauter* – literally, pull back in order to jump better. It sounds better in French.

Some branches of yoga and some of the more esoteric martial arts traditions such as Qi Gong and Shintaido focus on emptying the mind. A famous Qi Gong master once said to his pupils, "You think too much. Go to the zoo." We can learn a lot from watching animals and how they behave.

The more we still the mind, the more receptive we become to our intuition. Suspend the internal dialogue and you open the door to a serenity that empowers and energises.

Develop routines and schedules that include a period of solitude every day. Don't worry that you seem to be idle.

**Listen to your dreams – those are the sounds
no one else can hear.**
Kobe Yamada

That is the whole point. Idleness is essential. It gives space to dream, to contemplate, to wonder and to create. Book time with yourself to be yourself.

> It is not necessary that you leave the house. Remain at your table and listen. Do not even listen, only wait. Do not even wait, be wholly still and alone. The world will present itself to you for its unmasking … In ecstasy it will arrive at your feet.
> *Franz Kafka*

During these daily meditations, feed your subconscious mind with clear goals, great expectations and positive affirmations. Visualise your dreams as if they have come true.

Use your subconscious mind to solve problems and deliver answers and new ideas, by simply asking your subconscious mind before you meditate, then letting go. The answer may come directly, it may not. Whenever it comes, the timing will be right.

I've worked with numerous successful sports and business people who regularly schedule time in their diary to allow their body, mind and spirit to re-charge. I find that just five minutes at the beginning and end of each day is an incredibly powerful way to recalibrate the mind.

The calming influence of meditation makes your mind more

It is not what you are that holds you back, it is what you think you are not.
Denis Waitley

MIND, SET & MATCH

sensitive and subtle. In addition, it increases your power of concentration and your ability to see things objectively.

The philosophy behind meditation is simply explained by the Chinese Taoists. They tell us that energy is constantly being directed outward through the senses. Over time it becomes depleted. When we meditate we reverse the flow of energy, directing it back within ourselves, where it rejuvenates and replenishes us, mentally, physically and spiritually.

A well-educated man once went to a Zen master to enquire about the meaning of Zen. After greeting him, the master instructed the visitor to be seated and proceeded to pour him a cup of tea. The cup was filled, and still he poured. Tea spilled over the sides of the table and onto the floor, yet still the master poured. At last the visitor cried: "The cup is already full! It can hold no more!" The master replied "So it is. Just as you come to me – so full of what you know that you can receive nothing new."

All the wonders you seek are within yourself.
Thomas Brown

DIEt

One of the keys to personal fulfilment is balance in all areas of your life.

In my work as a psychotherapist I always found that whenever someone asked for help, some emotional or physical need was not being met. Like all animals, we need air to breathe, water to drink, nutritious food, shelter, sleep and freedom to stimulate our senses and exercise our bodies.

Like all animals, we intuitively know how much to eat and how much rest and exercise we need. However, many of us don't listen to our intuition. No wonder obesity is such an epidemic.

In the United States:
- obesity has overtaken tobacco as the biggest killer of people. Nearly 20% of all deaths in the US are currently attributed to obesity.
- From 1978 to 2008 the incidence of obesity more than doubled from 12% to 25%.
- Diseases such as diabetes have increased enormously in this period from 5 million to 20 million.

An inspired mind is of little use if you lack the physical vitality to execute your plans. Get active and get moving. Whether this means a daily exercise program or simply riding your bike to work, think of as many ways as possible to be active in your daily life.

In the time of your life – live!
William Shakespeare

MIND, SET & MATCH

Just as important as an active lifestyle is a healthy diet. You can't expect to have the energy and drive necessary to live an extraordinary life if you continue to fill your body with unhealthy foods. This doesn't mean that you have to give up ice cream and crisps, just that you eat such things in moderation as part of a lifelong practice of healthy eating. What you put in your body has an enormous impact on your motivation to improve.

Psychologists throughout the ages have determined that there are other needs, emotional rather than physical, which are equally crucial for our well-being. These include the need for:

- security – a safe territory, an environment where we can live without fear
- volition – a sense of autonomy and control
- attention – receiving it from others, but also giving it: essential nutrition for the healthy development of each individual, family and culture
- emotional connection to other people through friendship, love and intimacy
- community – humans are group animals and sanity is a group phenomenon. We need to know that we are part of something larger than ourselves
- privacy – time and space to reflect
- status – being accepted and valued in the various social groups that we belong to

Happiness is when what you say, what you think and what you do are in harmony.
Mahatma Gandhi

RESONATE

- a sense of our competence and achievement – which ensures that we don't develop low self-esteem
- being stretched in what we do and think – it's through 'stretching' ourselves mentally or physically (or both) that we learn and grow and our lives become purposeful and full of meaning

Use the list above to check how your emotional needs are being satisfied. Score yourself from 1 to 5, with 1 being 'not satisfied' and 5 being 'very satisfied'. Unless you score straight fives, you will see at a glance the areas where you need to act.

Man is so made that when anything fires his soul, impossibilities vanish.
Jean de La Fontaine

MIND, SET & MATCH

CHAPTER 7

THE CHILD RE-DISCOVERED

The Roaring Lion

The philosopher Friedrich Nietzsche described a three-stage process in the life of a human and the development of consciousness:

1 – Camel. In the first stage we are like a camel, where those around us force us to our knees so that they can pile upon us the burden of social conditioning, habit and convention.

2 – Lion. We reach a point in our lives where our innate desire to be free surfaces and we roar like a lion against the "shalls, musts, and shoulds" of society. Only after we have shown the courage to express our authentic selves and find our own path in life can we reach the third stage.

3 – Child. We are born free. As young children, we are carefree and unencumbered by social conditioning. We respond to the world spontaneously, intuitively and competently.

The critical stage in this process is that of the lion, where we challenge convention and break free from conditioning. Only then can we rediscover the child within. It's when we live with the heart of a child, but equipped with the capabilities of an adult, that we find true happiness and success.

During the course of this book, I hope I've demonstrated

Genius is nothing more or less than childhood recovered at will – a childhood now equipped for self-expression with an adult's capacities.

Charles Baudelaire

that success is not something to be chased. On the contrary, it is attracted to you because of the person that you become.

Once we realise our true identity, we will want to liberate others so that they too can create the life they want. When all is said and done, you're left with either results or excuses.

Only a life lived for others is a life worthwhile. A person starts to live when he can live outside of himself.
Albert Einstein

You Don't Walk Alone

There are four major life lessons I have learned, often the hard way, over the last 25 years.

Lesson 1

Everyone must take full responsibility for where they are in life. You must live your life free from excuses and blame.

Lesson 2

Life is about problems and challenges. These problems and challenges are your opportunity, not your excuses.

Lesson 3

Life is about giving. Takers lose and givers win. Once you get past asking "What's in it for me?" and start asking "How can I make your life happier?" your life will become infinitely richer and more meaningful. Life is about following your passion and giving your best. The more you give, the more you'll receive, period.

Keep moving, keep giving, keep living, so that the pages in the story of your life keep turning and you tell of the life wonderful life that you are now living.

Lesson 4

Have faith and trust in yourself and the world around you. You don't walk alone.

If you keep thinking the right thoughts and doing the right things, rest assured that you will live the life that you have dreamed of.

If you love and serve man you cannot, by any hiding or stratagem, escape remuneration.

Ralph Waldo Emerson

Today

Is anybody happier because you passed their way?
Does anyone remember that you spoke with them today?
Were you selfish, pure and simple, as you rushed along your way
Or is someone mighty grateful for a deed you did today?

Can you say tonight in passing with the day that's slipping past,
That you helped a single human in the many that you passed?
Is a single heart rejoicing over what you did or said?
Can a person whose hopes were fading now with courage look ahead?

Did you waste a day or lose it, was it well or poorly spent?
Did you leave a trail of kindness or a scar of discontent?
When you close your eyes in slumber, do you think your God will say,
You have earned one more tomorrow for the deeds you did today?

Max Hutching

Give more and you'll have more.
Hyrum W. Smith

CHAPTER 8

FINAL THOUGHTS

FINAL THOUGHTS

Quiz: Who Do You Remember?

The following is taken from the philosophy of Charles Schultz, the creator of the *Peanuts* comic strip. You don't have to answer the questions. Just read them, and you'll get the point.

1. Name the five wealthiest people in the world.

2. Name the five fastest men or women ever over 100m.

3. Name the people who have been voted the sexiest man and woman for each of the last three years.

4. Name ten people who have won a Nobel or Pulitzer Prize.

5. Name the last half dozen Academy Award winners for best actor and actress.

6. Name the last five winners of the World Cup.

How did you do?

The point is that none of us remember yesterday's headlines. These are not second rate achievers. They are the best in their field. But the applause dies. Awards tarnish. Achievements are forgotten. Accolades and certificates are buried with their owners.

Here's another quiz. See how you do on this one:

1. List the names of a few teachers who aided your journey through school.

The sole meaning of life is to serve humanity.
Tolstoy

MIND, SET & MATCH

2. Name three friends who have helped you through a difficult time.

3. Name five people who have taught you something worthwhile.

4. Think of a few people who have made you feel appreciated and special.

5. Think of five people you enjoy spending time with.

Easier?

The people who make a difference in your life are not the ones with the most credentials, the most money, or the most awards. They are the ones you care about.

The most sublime act is to set another before you.
William Blake

FINAL THOUGHTS

Love Is ...

A team of researchers asked a group of primary school children: "What does love mean?" The answers were broader and deeper than they could have imagined:

"When someone loves you, the way they say your name is different. You know that your name is safe in their mouth."
Billy, age 4

"Love is when you go out to eat and give somebody most of your French fries without making them give you any of theirs."
Chrissy, age 6

"Love is what makes you smile when you're tired."
Terri, age 4

"Love is what's in the room with you at Christmas if you stop opening presents and listen."
Bobby, age 7

"If you want to learn to love better, you should start with a friend who you hate."
Nikka, age 6

"During my piano recital I was on a stage and I was scared. I looked at all the people watching me and saw my daddy waving and smiling. He was the only one doing that. I wasn't scared anymore."
Cindy, age 8

**It is not who is right, but what is right,
that is of importance.**
Thomas Huxley

MIND, SET & MATCH

"Love is when Mummy gives Daddy the best piece of chicken."
Elaine, age 5

"Love is when Mummy sees Daddy smelly and sweaty and still says he is handsomer than Robert Redford."
Chris, age 7

"Love is when your puppy licks your face even after you left him alone all day."
Mary Ann, age 4

"I know my older sister loves me because she gives me all her old clothes and has to go out and buy new ones."
Lauren, age 4

"When you love somebody, your eyelashes go up and down and little stars come out of you."
Karen, age 7

"Love is when Mommy sees Daddy on the toilet and she doesn't think it's gross."
Mark, age 6

"You really shouldn't say 'I love you' unless you mean it. But if you mean it, you should say it a lot. People forget."
Jessica, age 8

Author and lecturer Leo Buscaglia once talked about a contest he was asked to judge. The purpose of the contest was to find the most caring child.

Person to person, moment to moment, as we love, we change the world.
Samaria Kaufman

FINAL THOUGHTS

The winner was a four-year-old whose next-door neighbour, an elderly gentleman, had recently lost his wife. Seeing the man cry, the little boy had gone into the old gentleman's yard, climbed onto his lap, and just sat there. When his mother asked him what he had said to the man, the little boy said, "Nothing, I just helped him to cry."

If you don't have love in your life, no matter what else there is, it's not enough.

Love really does make the world go round.

Each of us has a spark of life inside us, and our highest endeavour ought to be to set off that spark in one another.
Kenny Ausubel

Live Magically

On the surface we seem to be isolated individuals, But the latest findings in quantum physics increasingly support the notion that the whole universe is an interconnected web of energy.

When we're fully connected into the universal energy, we no longer see ourselves as limited, solitary beings. We realise that we are part of something fantastic and miraculous, and we can create whatever we want – and that makes us feel wonderful!

The way to connect and resonate with the universe is by expressing our uniqueness and living our DNA. In doing this we will inevitably enrich the lives of others. All that stands between you and your dreams is your own resistance. Have the courage to change your thinking, get out of you own way and let your light shine out.

Freedom comes from realising nothing 'out there' is responsible for what we experience or how we feel. Happiness is an inside job. The outer world simply mirrors our inner world.

Whatever happened in your past, the present moment is your point of power. The universe waits for you to ask for what you want.

Only you can say what you really, truly want. Your inner beacon is always on transmit, but you have to receive. Signals

May you live every day of your life.
Jonathan Swift

FINAL THOUGHTS

come in the form of emotional and intuitive impulses. Work on tuning your receiver and filtering out the noise. Trust your Inner Guidance System.

Choose authenticity over approval. Don't try to be good in the eyes of others. Live your own truth.

Choose to be happy. Chase your passion, not your pension. As we follow our passion, we reconnect with everyone and everything around us.

Pursue character before prosperity. Live with integrity, passion and a desire to make a difference to the lives of others and your dreams will come to you.

The universe is a conscious and benevolent entity. It always acts in your best interests and always brings into your life exactly what you need.

Think of a complicated trapeze act. The trapeze artiste lets go of the bar and thrills the audience with an array of twists and somersaults, and just as she finishes, the next bar is available for her to grasp. That's how the universe acts. The bar you need is always available when you need it. The choreography is both split-second and brilliant.

The lesson you need to learn is that you get exactly what you need, at exactly the minute you need it. The resources you need are made available at the precise time that it's appropriate. The people coming into your life are the very ones you need at the stage you're in.

Wheresoever you go, go with all your heart
Confucius

MIND, SET & MATCH

It is perfect.

It has always been perfect, but you just never saw this.

It will always be perfect in the future.

We are all born for love. It is the principle of our existence and its only end.
Benjamin Disraeli

Contact Sunil

... I would love to hear from you!

SUNIL BALI

PUREFORMANCE PUBLISHING

DUNCAN HOUSE

13 DUNCAN GROVE

SHENLEY CHURCH END

MILTON KEYNES, BUCKS

MK5 6HL

www.sunilbali.com

sunil@sunilbali.com